"The healing that you seek is not the healing of the body alone, but the return to the heart of God. I shall assist you in your healing. I am your friend and will be your guide should you ask me to walk with you on your pilgrimage through your past. As you move through your day, remember that the first step to feeling better is to allow yourself to feel."

— Archangel Raphael

This handbook is a companion. In its pages the Archangels Michael, Raphael, Gabriel, and Uriel have instilled their wisdom and love for mankind. Each Archangel, beginning with Saint Michael, will assist you with his respective area of responsibility.

With their guidance, you will process and learn from your current experiences and journey into the past. Along the way, you will meet unresolved hurts that must be reviewed, understood, expressed, accepted, and released. Each step takes you deeper to the source of all—toward the divine love current, your innocence, and possibly to the secrets of life and the universe.

The Archangels' plan of healing is sublime in its simplicity. Through the consistent application of various methods, you can achieve the state of angelic enlightenment. It does not require any degrees, certifications, initiations, or secret rituals. It is accomplished at your own pace by your own choice.

As you learn the the techniques of angelic enlightenment and begin to apply them even in small ways, changes will occur within you. As this happens, the world around you will begin to change as well. The act of self-love that you show yourself becomes an act of love for all humanity.

This is the Archangels' gift to us at the dawning of the new millennium. It is meant to show us the way back to our hearts.

About the Authors

Linda Miller-Russo is an accomplished spiritual reader who has an in-depth knowledge of human nature. She graduated Phi Beta Kappa from the University of Minnesota with a B.S. degree in Social Science. Linda loves to travel and has organized and led study tours in both Europe and the eastern United States. She has worked as a secondary teacher and as a social worker. This background provides her with an excellent repertoire of skills with which to assist you in accomplishing your life's mission.

Interpreting dreams has been Linda's passion for more than twenty-five years. Her abilities span lifetimes and are traced back to incarnations in ancient Egypt, Greece, and Persia where she served as a Dream Oracle. Presently, Linda unites her psychological training with the intuitive mystical elements brought forth from the wisdom pool of her higher self to provide dynamic and penetrating dream analysis for her clients.

Peter Miller-Russo has investigated spiritual subjects for more than twenty years and is a pioneer in modern-day astral travel and conscious-dream exploration. He is self-taught in computers, music, and graphic web-site design. Peter is proficient on both piano and guitar. His voice has a rich timbre and people often compliment him on his singing abilities. He has performed both in public and at spiritual workshops.

Commissioned by the Archangel Michael in 1994, Peter's mission as a Bearer of the Sword of Truth is to weave the truth of spirit into words and melodies that help bring the awareness of peace and divine understanding into your life. In composing Soul Name Songs™ (a genre that he created) he is able to access information from the wisdom pool of the higher self to channel words and melodies into Soul Name Songs for individuals. His intuitive insight into the human and divine can help empower you to fulfill your chosen destiny.

The Circle Of Angelic Enlightenment was founded by Linda and Peter and is dedicated to assisting each individual in their efforts to define and accomplish their life's mission. Through the inspiration and guidance of the Angels and the Archangels, Linda and Peter present the Archangels' Plan of Healing through books, tapes, Soul Name Songs, dream interpretations, and past life regressions. Also offered is the Circle of Angels' discourse study/membership program. It is an ongoing, monthly home-study program geared to fully empower you to complete your life's mission. The first year is entitled: Reawakening the Inner Self.

For information on these services, the study/membership program, speaking engagements, or private sessions, Linda and Peter can be contacted directly by writing to:

Linda and Peter Miller-Russo
The Circle of Angelic Enlightenment
P.O. Box 322
Cottage Grove, MN. 55016
Email: info@angelic-circle.com   Web Site: www.angelic-circle.com

Please include a self-addressed, stamped envelope for reply; or to receive the
Circle of Angelic Enlightenment's full color catalog, please enclose $1.00 to cover costs.

Linda & Peter Miller-Russo

Angelic Enlightenment

A Personal Process

1999
Llewellyn Publications
St. Paul, Minnesota 55164-0383

FIRST EDITION
First Printing, 1999

Cover design by Lisa Novak
Editing and interior design by Astrid Sandell

Library of Congress Cataloging-in-Publication Data
Miller-Russo, Linda, 1956–
    Angelic Enlightenment : a personal process / Linda & Peter Miller-Russo.
  — 1st ed.
      p.   cm.
    Includes index
    ISBN 1-56718-482-0
    1. Archangels—Miscellanea. 2. Spiritual Life. I. Miller-Russo,
Peter, 1957– II. Title.
    BF1999.M685 19999
    291.2'15—dc21   99-22349
                                    CIP

Llewellyn Publications
A Division of Llewellyn Worldwide, Ltd.
P.O. Box 64383, Dept. K482-0,
St. Paul, MN 55164-0383

Printed in the United States of America

Dedication

This book is dedicated with special care to the Archangels' Plan of Healing for Mankind as revealed to us by the four Archangels: Michael, Raphael, Gabriel, and Uriel. Through their guidance and care we have found peace, understanding, and growth. May peace and enlightenment fill your lives and may the Angels guide and inspire you always.

Acknowledgments

The Circle of Angelic Enlightenment was founded through the inspiration of the four Archangels: Michael, Raphael, Gabriel, and Uriel. These four Archangels form the foundation of the Circle of Angels. We thank them for their guidance.

We also want to thank the following people for their roles in bringing us together:

Rev. Carolyn White, our good friend—for her acceptance,
unconditional love, and support.

Rev. Carol Parrish and Rev. Tom Hyder—for their inspirational
wisdom teachings, and their reverence for each individual's link with the divine.

Kate (Lightwalker), Liz (of WE), Melissa (for the channeling session at the WE
event), Sandra (spiritual reader), Kurt, Karol, Rae, and Mary.

And our family and friends, for their positive thoughts, love, and support.

And these are the names of the holy angels who watch.
Uriel, one of the holy angels, who is over the world and over Tartarus.
Raphael, one of the holy angels, who is over the spirits of men . . .
Michael, one of the holy angels, to wit, he that is set over the best part
of mankind and over chaos . . .
Gabriel, one of the holy angels, who is over Paradise
and the serpents and the Cherubim . . .

—Enoch I: 1–8

Contents

Introduction

A Message from Peter

ONLY A FEW times during our life does a window of expanded consciousness open up to our awareness. At these times, we see the truth of life with a clarity enlivened by the life-giving essence of the Holy Spirit. It imbues our life and we see ourselves as a complete being, at one with the universe and all its creations.

At these times we are faced with ourselves. We are willing and eager to look into our mind, soul, and heart—not with fear but with love. Unstoppable is our desire to strip away the illusions from our eyes, and to address the conditioning we have accepted as reality.

In the summer and autumn of 1994, such a cycle of expanded consciousness began for me. I was blessed by the presence and loving energy of Saint Michael the Archangel. He guided my mind and heart to the part of me hidden from the world. It still existed, but was buried deep within me from years of repression in a failed marriage and my involvement in a spiritual path within which I had cloaked myself.

As the casing of my old life was shedding, a new life was emerging. This spiritual emergence was an outcropping of this expansion of consciousness. All things were possible once again for me as life regained its mystery and wonder. I became alive for the first time in many years, alive in the Holy Spirit. Not in my mind only, but in my whole being.

This time was marked by my first meeting with Linda in September, 1994. Events converged at the first WE (Walk-ins for Evolution) conference in St. Paul, Minnesota. A circle was formed as Linda and I met to fulfill our destiny in the service of the Angels and the Creator.

Michael visited me in my dreams shortly after that conference to impress upon me aspects of my mission to come. The first was to bring into complete manifestation the powers of discernment from my soul self into the conscious world. With this awareness, I would be able to see into the motivations of myself and others. As a bearer of "The Sword of Truth" I accepted the responsibility of viewing the truth of all that I had contributed to this world.

The next aspect of my mission was to heal the old emotional wounds of my past—this lifetime, and possibly others. I began to clear the protections from around my heart, which I had used to deaden the pain and starkness of my life.

Once you become aware that you are living—here and now—the dual realization comes to you that you will someday pass away—pass away from those whom you love and from those whom you care for, perhaps never to see them again. It is this eternal play of God's energy and plan that most people find hard to accept. It means that we must trust; painful experiences from the past make trusting a frightening prospect.

The child within, with its tender self, has been so hurt by life that it finds it very difficult to trust the world again. But trust it must, and trust *you* must, if you wish to accelerate your growth and take steps to fulfill your life's mission—your reason for being. Raphael came to me as an energy of healing from the shattering experiences of the past that had driven me into a crippled emotional shell. I had come to reject the emotions as negative, and for many years I considered them not spiritual. Raphael has helped me learn to accept my emotions as a blessed part of myself to be cherished, understood, expressed, and then released. For this I thank him daily.

Since life is a process, I continue to strive to be honest with myself and to accurately label and express my emotions when I feel them; to find the deeper emotion at the core of the energy stream emanating from the emotion. Doing this assists me in maintaining relationships of complete and conscious honesty with myself and my loved ones.

As I struggled through the years 1995 and 1996, I began to gain strength of purpose and clarity of thought. Linda and I would have long talks at our favorite coffeehouse several times a week. We explored spiritual concepts, the Angels, the emotions, religion, cults, psychology, whatever we were currently experiencing and had learned in this lifetime. The growth that comes from being with another is one of God's greatest gifts, and I thank Linda for loving me, and for her patience in discussing all of the past painful experiences of my life. Her insights were helpful and healing.

Through these talks, we gathered many concepts and wrote most of them down in journals as we spoke. A pattern was developing. We could see the path of the

Angels, the path to angelic enlightenment forming before our eyes. With the help of the strengthening energy of Gabriel, we were able to take action to bring forth the Archangels' message of healing to humanity at the dawn of the Aquarian age.

I am continuing to work closely with the Archangel Gabriel. As this mission unfolds, I promise to commit myself to the Archangels' plan of healing and angelic enlightenment. I will persist with my life's mission outwardly and continue to process my day-to-day experiences to keep my heart open inwardly. I will try to bravely face the experiences of my past in order to gain understanding and cultivate wisdom. I desire to increase my capacity to love; to accept God's love and to let it flow through my heart.

During my journey I have come to realize that Uriel, the Archangel of love, beauty, and appreciation has been beside me all along. Like a loving father, he has watched as Michael, Raphael, and Gabriel have worked with me toward angelic enlightenment. I look forward to completing my mission, to cleanse and heal myself, and to experience the loving help of Uriel more and more as time goes by. I feel that the culmination of learning that this Archangel is assisting me with will complete the cycle of angelic enlightenment that I began in 1994. I hope to continue to spread the love of the Archangels, and of myself, to others and to the world.

May peace, growth, love, and understanding grace your life and those of your loved ones, and may you find that which you desire.

With loving kindness,
Peter Miller-Russo

A Message from Linda

As a child, I was always encouraged to examine the mysteries of life. Mealtime conversations with the family often centered on the miracles of the saints, life after death, the Virgin Mary apparitions, and dreams of angels or spiritual beings. Nurtured in an atmosphere of possibilities and simple faith, I learned to believe and trust in the presence and care of Jesus, the angels, and the saints.

Sometimes I can feel or "sense" the presence of angels and light beings. I believe this sensing ability evolved naturally from the attitude of reverence for spirituality fostered within my family, and from the deep connection to nature that I learned from growing up on a farm. On warm summer days, I would often walk to a clearing in the middle of the woods, sit beneath my favorite pine tree, close my eyes, and just be. I would breathe in the fresh pine scent and listen to the hum of the insects and the calling of the birds. All of life seemed connected—the earth was our mother.

My father is a great storyteller. He would often spark my imagination by telling tales of giants, elves, brownies, and leprechauns. He knew about my sojourns into the woods and he would advise me to "just sit as quietly as you can, listen carefully, be very still. Soon creatures of all kinds will become visible to you—squirrels, striped gophers, porcupines . . . and if you're lucky maybe even a brownie or an elf will come out of hiding for you."

Life on the farm was simple, yet rich with possibilities. I read every book I could get my hands on, and sometimes co-wrote short stories and poems with my next door neighbor and best friend, Phyllis. As children, we used our powerful imaginations to become various nature beings, ranging from the mythological Pegasus (winged horse) to creatures of the Faerie Kingdom. It was always a jolt to be called out of that glorious world to help with some chore on the farm!

During my adolescence, prayer and informal meditations in nature continued to connect me with the spiritual world and with my own higher self. It was during this time (about age seventeen) when I had my first "remembrance" of a past-life that I had lived in the New England area. Two years earlier, I had studied reincarnation and karma in a world religion class. Although the concepts were not part of my religious upbringing, they made sense and "felt" true to me. I decided to incorporate them into my personal philosophy of how the world probably worked. Later on, in adulthood, I had several spiritual readings and past-life regressions that seemed to confirm the details of the "remembrances" I had experienced in my adolescence.

Over the next twenty years, I continued to expand, study, and grow—learning as much as I could about the disciplines of both psychology and spirituality. My friend Mary and I would often do spiritual readings and dream interpretations for each other. Through this process, I learned about universal as well as personal symbols.

In the fall of 1993, I made a commitment to concentrate on my spirituality and to uncover my personal mission. I connected with like-minded spiritual seekers and immersed myself in spiritual studies, daily meditations, healing, and intuitive development classes. I learned to consciously invoke (invite) the angels, Archangels, and spiritual guides to assist me in bringing the complete truth into my relation-ships, healing my emotional/etheric bodies, and in uncovering my mission.

In the spring and summer of 1994, I was working closely with the Archangel Uriel on the transformational process of accepting and appreciating the beauty of humanity's divine nature. I was learning how to listen to the wisdom of my higher self and to bring forth that wisdom into my everyday actions. Early on a sunny June morning in 1994, I came to the realization that the butterfly was not just a universal symbol of transformation, but that it was also the personal sign or symbol that my higher self used to confirm to me that I had made the right decision.

On that particular June morning, around 7A.M., I was about to leave for work. My mind was preoccupied with many details because I was leaving the state the next day for a week-long spiritual retreat. I was excited and apprehensive—if all went well, I planned on formally entering a ministerial program during that week. I left the house with this decision heavy on my mind (Would I be able to afford the tuition? Would my car hold up on the long trips to the seminary?), when I nearly stumbled on a huge butterfly. I couldn't believe my eyes. On the ground in front of me (in my direct path) was a beautiful monarch butterfly with a wingspan of at least twelve inches.

I couldn't believe it! Butterflies are small in Minnesota—I'd never seen one before with a wingspan any greater than three inches. Nevertheless, there it was. I couldn't leave it on the path because my neighbor might step on it. So I found a piece of cardboard and slid it underneath the butterfly. It fluttered its wings as I gently moved it (it was heavy for a butterfly) to a safe spot on the lawn. It was hard to concentrate on work that day as I thought about what this might mean. I felt it must be the sign that I had been asking my higher self for—the sign that I had made the right decision to join the seminary. As the day wore on, I began to question myself. Perhaps I had imagined the enormous size of this butterfly? I decided to put it out of my mind—I had paperwork to prepare and several client meetings to attend later that afternoon.

By the time I left for home that night, work issues had driven all thoughts of the butterfly out of my mind. But as I drove up to the garage, I noticed something orange in the direct path of my front left tire. I got out of the car and, to my amazement, there it was again! As huge as ever, the butterfly was perched directly in front of my tire. There was no way I could miss this sign. Again I moved the butterfly to safety, and gave thanks for this second confirmation from my higher self.

Since that experience in 1994, I consciously ask my higher self to signal me if I am on the right track by sending a butterfly sign. Each time the butterfly sign arrives, it comes in a new way (in a new form) that I did not anticipate. Sometimes the butterfly comes in dreams; sometimes it is a butterfly gift that someone unexpectedly gives me. Most recently it came in the form of a beautiful painting of a butterfly. At these times, I feel the energy of the Archangel Uriel, who seems to facilitate my connection to my higher self and assists me in increasing my awareness and appreciation for the beauty and divinity present in humanity and in the world at large.

I give thanks daily for the gift of my family and friends, the gift that the farm has been to me, and for my husband Peter who was definitely the spark-plug for this project. I thank him for his tremendous energy, enthusiasm, and vision.

May this book inspire growth within you, and may the Angels' loving presence become a waking reality in your life.

In the spirit of light and love,
Linda Miller-Russo

The Archangels' Plan of Healing for Mankind

For He shall give his Angels
charge over you
To keep you in all your ways.
In their hands, they shall bear you up,
lest you dash your foot against a stone.

—Psalms 91:11–12

1

Life is a Process, Not a Result

LIFE IS A process, not a result. *Angelic Enlightenment: A Personal Process* is a guide. This book will help you learn how to process your day-to-day experiences in a way that assists the energy centers in your body to flow in healing and peaceful patterns.

Most, if not all problems in life come when we do not take the time to process or learn from our experiences. When we take the time to learn by applying constructive ways to process our experiences, we find that life becomes more joyful and fulfilling because we actually feel the love and joy that is our nature. This comes in part from the state of honesty that effective processing requires.

The love and joy of our higher self has been pushed down by the experiences of this world that hurt us. These experiences have crippled our ability to deal with our pain. Every time that you were rejected, your loving self became more and more hidden within you. "To be as the little child," as Jesus said, is to be as the higher self. To be as the higher self is to live in the state of love and joy that is your natural state of being.

But how can you achieve your natural state of being again? Have you actually lost contact with that state? Most of us have, to some degree or another at different times in our lives, lost contact with that natural state of being. Haven't you ever longed to experience a time in your life from the past? Will that state return to you someday by chance? Are you content to leave it to destiny, never knowing where the winds of life will blow you tomorrow?

Consider the possibility that you could live your life imbued with feelings of joy and love every day—feelings that make life truly worth living. What would you do to achieve that? This book contains the way to achieve that state, in a consistent and direct manner. No longer will you be spiritual simply because you are supposed to be according to your religion or spiritual path, but rather because you will actually be feeling the love that is you! As the ancients, inspired by the Angels, have said, "Man know thyself." This statement is as true today as it was millenniums ago.

The Archangels Michael, Raphael, Gabriel, and Uriel have instilled their wisdom and love for mankind in the pages of this book. This is their gift to us at the dawning of the new millennium. It is a guide to angelic enlightenment; it is meant to show us the way to our hearts again. This is what the age of Aquarius is all about—self-mastery by healing our hearts to allow our higher self to shine through every energy center of our being.

The Archangels' gift to us came at a time when we desperately needed it. Perhaps this knowledge is here for you now to help you at a time in your life when you also need it. We thank the Archangels for their help and guidance.

The Archangels' Plan

The Archangels' plan of healing for mankind is a process. It flows through the divine energies of the four Archangels. Each has a specific purpose and specific powers to assist you in attaining angelic enlightenment.

The Archangels are known by different names in the various world religions; this book refers to them by the names known to the Christian western world. In brief, the four Archangels and their main power, purpose, and process segments are shown below. The purpose, power, and process of each Archangel is explored in greater depth in sections two through five.

Archangel	Purpose	Main Power	Process
Saint Michael	truth, honesty, justice	seeing	understanding
Saint Raphael	healing, wholeness, acceptance	feeling	expressing
Saint Gabriel	strength, persistence, commitment	acting	accomplishment
Saint Uriel	love, beauty, awareness	being	appreciation

Through the guidance of each of the four Archangels we are led on a journey. This journey culminates in a greater understanding of ourselves and our inherent spirituality. In succession, and at times concurrently, each of the Archangels introduce into our energy stream a particular vibration. This vibration helps us move into new cycles and energy patterns. The new patterns present us with opportunities to choose other cycles of experience. These cycles will accelerate our growth through the education of the self in the art of living.

As we willingly let go of old patterns and heal the emotional wounds of the past, we begin to realize that what we were doing before was not really living, it was just existing. Living life with purpose is the difference between really *living* and just existing.

As the Archangels' plan of healing begins to work in our lives, we start receiving glimpses of purity and light that fill our hearts with joy and excitement. Just as breaks in the clouds allow the sun's rays to warm our body on a cold day, so too do the rays of divine energy warm our souls as we see glimpses of the inner innocence of our child within. The Archangels' plan of healing is primarily a method to process our daily experiences in a way that allows our hearts to remain open to the divine in purity and innocence. This is our original state.

As Within, As Without

This world is a laboratory of soul. We have come to earth to grow through experience in the worlds of matter, energy, space, and time. Part of what we learn here is how to effectively process the experiences that occur in our lives. The purpose in processing our experiences is twofold. First, we process to learn from the experience and to integrate its knowledge into our being. Second, we process in order to remain in touch with our connection to the divine and to the life stream known as the Holy Spirit.

In order to create change, we need to identify the unconscious patterns that have become a part of us. This requires us to honestly view our current life situation. Next, we must express any unresolved feelings that have been generated during the past as we became who we are now. After expression comes acceptance of the experience as a whole, and finally there is the release of the experience cycle as the knowledge has been integrated into our conscious self for use in this life.

By choosing to focus on understanding the influences that have come to shape our lives, we are led on a journey—a journey to ourselves. Our immediate surroundings are vital clues to the self that we are. As we process our experiences in the present by viewing our current circumstances, we are led on a journey to the past. Along the way, guided by the four Archangels, we meet unresolved hurts that must be reviewed, understood, expressed, accepted, and released. Each step takes us deeper to the source of all—toward the divine love current, our innocence, and possibly to the secrets of life and the universe.

This book is a companion. In it, each Archangel, beginning with Saint Michael, will assist you with their respective area of responsibility. The Archangels do this with their knowledge, understanding, and love for mankind and for you. Their ways are always healing and supportive and address all aspects of the self, including the basic/subconscious self and the shadow self that hides within it. They communicate with us through such means as dreams, intuition, direct perception, visions, and channeled messages.

We have found that the process of angelic enlightenment is not without pain. But remember that this pain is not from the Archangels nor from the process of enlightenment itself—rather it is from the experiences of your life that you are now facing in truth and honesty, with a desire to learn and grow.

The Archangels' plan of healing for mankind is sublime in its simplicity. Through the consistent application of various methodologies and a desire to be, one can achieve the state of angelic enlightenment. This is accomplished at one's own pace by one's own choice alone. It does not require degrees or certification. Nor does it require initiation or secret rituals.

What the Archangels' plan requires of you is honesty, acceptance, commitment, and love. These Godly attributes are within the self that you are. As you learn the techniques of angelic enlightenment and begin to apply them to your life, even in small ways, changes will begin to occur within you. As changes occur within you, the choices that you make begin to change the world around you. As within, as without. The act of self-love that you show yourself becomes an act of love for all humanity. In this way, you are living in the microcosm and the macrocosm simultaneously. You have achieved the state of balance spoken of by the Buddha and you live in the state of compassion of the Christ.

The honesty that we write about refers to self-honesty—knowing one's self. Acceptance refers to the true definition of detachment, which is accepting the reality of one's situation and circumstances as they are here and now. Commitment means turning the corner on complacency. It is taking the time to remember the priorities in our life and motivating ourselves to continue with our life's mission. Finally, the Archangels' plan requires you to love. This divine aspect flowers within you, blossoming without fail, as you attain the state of angelic enlightenment.

Now all this may sound like a great deal of work—self-work—and it is. That is where the commitment comes in. But you will find as you begin the process of self-discovery that life becomes full of wonder again. You will have taken the steps to reclaim your spiritual heritage. And the beauty of this process is that you can finally be *you!*

No longer will you need to deny the shadow self—that part of the light that became darkness. You will be able to feel whatever it is you are feeling without censure that you are not spiritual. To deny the self and your experiences is to reject life itself, but to accept the self and your experiences is spirituality in action.

It may take you a while to be able to view yourself and your actions without automatically censoring and rationalizing your experiences to fit a particular belief system. With practice you will learn to allow more and more of the truth of yourself to be viewed as each day unfolds. You will come to "know thyself."

Don't confuse releasing your problems with releasing your will,
or accepting the absurd. Forgive and embrace yourself.
Return to the past to find out why you chose the road you did.

2

A Message from the Four Archangels

What is the Archangels' Plan of Healing?

As men and women in the physical world, you are driven to seek pleasure and to avoid pain. Your nature is to feel. To ignore your feelings is to deny the self, and to deny the self is to cover your pain for unsealing at a later time. To ignore your feelings is to deny the experience you have yourselves chosen—it is to dishonor the self.

On the contrary, if you choose to revel in your feelings; to imbue your life with the honesty of self-examination; to take the chance to change the situations you find yourself in for the better—if that is your choice, then you will have chosen to live a life of discovery, excitement, wonder, and peace.

Love, of itself, is not intended to be used as a bandage to cover your wounds—rather it is the water of life with which you cleanse your wounds. Cleanse your wounds with the water of love, the clear light of being—devoid of concepts, or the need of these concepts. Then you will see the self that shines all around and within you.

You will find that love is the attribute of BEING in total honesty to yourself. The harmonics of honesty will resonate the light of the divine being. Consciousness consists of the immediate realization of the life force. It is in part an awareness of the environment you exist in at this moment and the worlds you choose to place your attention on at this moment. By changing your attitude, you change your destiny.

The Angels are not bandages to cover your pain. Their purpose is not to act as shields to hide yourself behind. Nor are they a commodity to control others at man's will. The Angels are messengers of God and facilitators of healing and growth.

You will likely not find much peace in this world if you fail to find peace with your choices. You will be unable to consistently give peace in this world if you do not cleanse yourself with the water of life—love. By using the harmonics of honesty to allow your higher self to shine above you, and through you, you will bring peace into manifestation, and your choices will be made from clarity rather than through dysfunction.

We, the four Archangels, have chosen to bring this plan of healing to mankind because of our love for all of humanity. We have chosen to continue the pattern of honesty, sending the currents of conscious loving through all the worlds of God.

The plan of healing urges you to follow the trail of your own desires to find the truth of your own being! Desire is the source of all growth. It is the root position from which man and woman may proceed to know themselves. To know yourself is to know the self. It is the starting point for everything that you desire.

The Angels and the Archangels have chosen to share this message with you, through the selves that we are, in order to cultivate greater clarity, light, and love for all beings. Now it is your choice to choose the harmonics of honesty, to face the fictions you have erected as protective barriers, and to heal your hearts, with the clarity of seeing, and the pure light of being.

God is the only initiator, the first cause from which all life has flowed. Manifestations of God, the first cause, and the Angels are all around you. It is not man that initiates. No being needs to connect your heart with God's heart, for you are already connected to the Creator, heart to heart, in pure energy beyond all concepts and measurements.

God is the force that lights the universe with love and being. The Archangels' plan exhorts you to heal with the water of life; love. It asks you to cleanse your wounds and live with the wonder of the child within.

God is the pure energy that vibrates in your soul, that pulses within you with each beat of your heart, that builds and transmutes worlds, forms, and substances. What is the voice you feel within you? It is your higher self. The self that is our self. The Archangels' plan instructs you to connect to your higher self by following the trail of your desires to the source of your pain and to heal yourself with the waters of life—love.

The wisdom that comes from the study of the Archangels is reflected in a deeper understanding of the universal design of life. It comes with a commitment from you to total self-honesty and childlike trust in the Creator.

The design of your nature as men and women is to flow with the energy of God's universe. There is no true static state. Everything is always moving and always vibrating. Never ceasing is the call of your soul. And never have you been separated from the divine Creator.

The secret of God's existence lies in the DUALITY of the world in which you live. Those of you who would try to uncover this knowledge should start first with your own desires. You then follow them to find their true motivations. The Angels ask you again to examine your values and your belief systems if you sincerely wish to attain angelic enlightenment.

Belief systems are only slices of God as a complete being. You can enjoy them for what they provide for you. You learn from what you believe and then discard certain beliefs as you learn more. You live and then you grow. You love and then you come to know.

The Archangels' plan of healing explains that you have free will; you have always had free will. By choosing to process your experiences as we instruct, you allow the flow of Spirit to move through your bodies unimpeded by restrictions arising from the fears within you.

God is of one energy—combined in various ways for your experience and pleasure. If you do not wish to believe something, you must first discover what your beliefs are and then understand how they were formed.

At one time belief is based on faith. At another, it is based on proof. And at the root, they are both based on assumptions. These assumptions are based on your experiences. And on top of your experiences you create assumptions about God's divine being.

Yet we tell you that your assumptions do not affect the reality that is, but only the reality that you are aware of. If you wish to live a life of assumptions, then why did you take embodiment as a form of experience? The worlds that you live in are created for you to live in, now!

So process your experiences now. You wait because you feel that you would incur more pain by processing your experiences than by ignoring them. But you forget the real meaning of karma. It is the cycle of experience that soul chooses. It is the displacement of energy within the world and the experiencing of the flow of that energy.

The Archangels wish for you to challenge life and yourself! To rise up and challenge the elements. To question, to search, and to grow. We believe in you and we await you in the sanctity of your heart. We are invisible to the eyes of the body, but are not hidden to the soul who moves in truth; to one who allows divine energy to move through the centers of their being because they have learned how to process their experiences.

Truth is the all-encompassing wholeness of everything. Once you attempt to define God's nature, you split off from the whole. Stop! Learn! Listen! It is the Lord who gives thee life. Come live again. Rise up against the yoke of complacency, of mediocrity, of despondency, and empower yourselves to complete thy earthly purpose and mission.

We will teach you how to process your experiences. With this ability you will find that your experiences take on more vibrancy and light; you become filled with the unimpeded peace of divine energy.

Wisdom, power, and love are yours not based on membership in secret and non-secret organizations, nor through special initiations controlled and dispensed to you from outside of yourself. Wisdom, power, and love are yours simply because you choose to recognize and accept them—and have removed your masks and protective barriers that keep you from these Godly attributes.

Acceptance is a step toward conscious integration with Spirit. For why else did you come to earth to experience? Except to learn. If you choose not to process your experiences you lose the full benefit of them. Is that your desire? Do you not love yourself as the Angels love you?

Desire is the source of all growth, and as shall be explained, it is intertwined with experiencing the earth world. By breaking the hold of your conditioning you can become aware of that which has always been. Lasting peace and happiness are yours as you live in the purity of self-truth; the truth of living in the present of what you are actually feeling—love and hate, anger and peace, pain and pleasure. Understanding your motivations, uncovering your values and why you believe what you do is of critical importance.

Central to the Archangels' plan of healing is to explore the emotions that you feel and then learn to properly label them. It is most important to note that the emotions are given to you not as a hindrance, but as a valuable tool to enhance your experience of the worlds you have chosen to inhabit.

The Angels teach that there are no right or wrong emotions! There are only emotions. What you feel in a situation is simply your feeling. You can grab hold of the energy of the emotion and follow the chain of energy deeper to the source.

The root emotion is where you will find the greatest learning and the most tender part of yourself that you may have lost conscious contact with. The root emotion will lead you to other causes and you will see the patterns that have shaped your values and beliefs, which in turn have narrowed the scope of your available experiences by focusing your attention on a small sliver of creation.

We invite you to begin a journey of self-honesty by facing your deepest fears! In your heart lies the truth—hidden behind walls of fear. We, the four Archangels, send our love to you to empower you to help yourself.

May you find peace, understanding, and the courage to live your life with truth, honesty, and appreciation for all.

In the light and love of the Creator, we are always with you.

—Michael, Raphael, Gabriel, and Uriel

There is no proof, there is only experience, belief, and faith.

3

The Five Segments of the Self and the Seven Keys to Self-Knowledge

FOR DISCUSSION PURPOSES, we divide the integrated human into five segments. These five segments are: the soul self, the higher self, the emotional self, the basic/subconscious self, and the conscious/intellectual self. Through the integration of each self, in full awareness, we come to gain each of the seven keys to self-knowledge. We have followed the advice of the ancients and have come to "know thyself."

The Five Segments of the Self

1. The Soul Self
2. The Higher Self
3. The Emotional Self
4. The Basic/Subconscious Self
5. The Conscious/Intellectual Self

Segment One. The Soul Self: Indestructible Atom of God

Soul is the key component of the self. It is imperishable, composed of pure Spirit. Soul has a design of its own intent and a purpose behind its choice to extend itself into the world of embodiments for experience. When all the selves are integrated, a state of soul infusion exists within the individual. Some confuse the waking self with the soul self. The soul self is not the waking self. The soul self is that spiritual voice within you that carries a vibration of immense love and well-being. It knows no fear nor hunger nor darkness and decay.

As a particle of God, the soul self has the free will to explore at its discretion the worlds of spirit and the worlds of matter. It is said that the soul self can have multiple existences simultaneously in multiple worlds, physical and non-physical. Therefore it is possible for the soul to be gaining experience from several embodiments at the same time. The conscious self is not aware of these other embodiments—nor does it need to be.

Segment Two. The Higher Self: Our Wisdom Pool

The higher self is the repository of earthly experience culled from the myriad of sensory inputs of man as a being. In order to fulfill the soul's purpose for this life we, as the conscious mind, attempt to connect to the wisdom of the higher self and draw on this knowledge to assist us in our day-to-day life.

Our higher self can be reached through meditation and the God-given faculty of the imagination. The higher self is a vessel of Spirit that stores the wisdom gained in our cumulative life experiences. The soul self spins the conscious self, the personality, into existence in the physical worlds of matter, energy, space, and time. The higher self acts as a conduit between the conscious self and the soul self.

Segment Three. The Emotional Self: Guide to the Truth

Our emotional self attempts to give us guidance in the form of reactive clues from our day-to-day experiences at work or at home, with co-workers or loved ones. By learning to understand and work along with the emotional self, we can keep the basic self from working overtime in its attempts to reach our conscious self.

Usually maligned by many as negative, the emotional self is a key component of the integrated human being, which provides a very real and very needed function. It tells us when we need to act and points us in the direction of greater healing. To ignore its messages is to miss vital clues for keeping our heart and mind open to the Holy Spirit in love and goodwill.

The ability to feel the emotions, as experienced by the emotional self, is a God-given faculty, similar in importance to the imagination, which when understood by the conscious/intellectual self, is seen to be an invaluable tool in living our lives with an open heart.

Segment Four. The Basic/Subconscious Self: The Child Within

At the same time that our conscious self is striving to balance all the factors of modern life, we are constantly receiving impulses from our basic self (the subconscious self). These impulses come in the form of strong feelings, instinctual urges, and dreams.

The shadow self forms part of our basic self. It is the part of ourselves that was light and became the darkness in order to serve in our own unfoldment. It is the hurt part of ourselves whose protective, survival-oriented (unconscious) defense mechanisms we no longer need. The shadow self can be brought back to into the light—understood, healed, and released.

The basic self is concerned with survival. This means physical, emotional, and intellectual survival. It is sometimes primitive in its imaging. We embrace and honor it for the valuable function that it provides—our connection to the earth world and the elements of earth, air, water, and fire—and our continued survival in this world.

A problem here is that the basic self alone is not equipped with the necessary components to accurately judge the experiences of the conscious self. When we predominately react to life from the basic self, our actions become survival-oriented. This instinct for survival obviously has a purpose—physical and psychological well-being are requirements for one to exist on the physical plane and interact with the environment—but if the basic self is allowed to run the show, so to speak, we run the risk of reverting to existence at the level of the animal kingdom.

No state of consciousness is permanent in the sense that we must remain in it indefinitely. The energy of the universe is fluid and dynamic. We are in a sea of God's energy. If we find ourselves stuck in a pattern or experience that we find intolerable, there is help. Usually you can help yourself out of an unwanted pattern by using one or more of the methodologies described in this book, particularly the L.E.A.R.N. technique presented in chapter 15.

Segment Five. The Conscious/Intellectual Self: The Waking Personality

The conscious self is the state that we can most easily identify with. It is the waking personality that the world knows us by. It is also how the soul's pattern for this life has worked itself down into the matter worlds. Remember that the soul self spins the personality into the earth worlds. That personality is a major part of the waking self (the conscious self).

The personality consists of our values, likes and dislikes, and general attitudes toward various subjects (our beliefs). It is built by the environmental factors encountered while growing up, as well by the hereditary factors of genetics. Both these factors are part of the building blocks that the soul self uses when spinning the personality into existence. In order to move the conscious self into areas of experience as desired, the soul self fashions the embodiment of the conscious self.

As we, the conscious self, learn more about our complete makeup and the five self-segments, we begin to align our self to the Holy Spirit and our life's mission. We come to understand and integrate soul's pattern for this life. We enter the state of soul infusion where we are alive with divine energy in all the segments of the self.

The Seven Keys to Self-Knowledge

In addition to understanding the five segments of the self, we need to study the following seven keys to self-knowledge. By viewing the information that comes when we focus on each of the keys, we gain an awareness and understanding of our internal processes. The seven keys to self-knowledge are:

1. Understanding your dreams
2. Understanding your feelings
3. Understanding your thought patterns
4. Understanding your body
5. Understanding your desires
6. Understanding your shadow self
7. Understanding your mortality

Key One: *Understanding Your Dreams*

Dreams sometimes contain messages from the basic self. These messages from the basic self are at the direction of the soul self. At other times, dreams contain information from the wisdom pool of the higher self. When we come to understand our dreams, we gain the internal and experiential knowledge of how our basic self operates to provide us with input about significant areas of our life.

Dream experiences, as explained in chapter 4, are just as valid as the experiences of our day-to-day life. It is in the processing of our experiences—dreams or otherwise—that we gain insight and eventual wisdom.

The first step to understanding your dreams is to remember them! If you are having trouble remembering your dreams, make sure you are getting enough rest. If that does not help, try changing your sleep position so that your head points north and your feet point south. Experiment until you can access your dream memories. Staying in bed upon first awakening and gently "recalling" can help you travel down the reverse thread of a dream. Often, recalling one detail of a dream will trigger more memories to arise within you. Dream symbols are discussed in more detail in chapter 27.

Key Two: Understanding Your Feelings

Feelings and emotions have swayed men and women since time began. Many of us have been taught (especially in some of the "new age" paths) that our emotions are negative and lacking in spirituality. The Circle of Angelic Enlightenment teaches that each and every part of ourselves (the self-segments) is a holy part—deserving of honor and respect. Respect is given when we focus our attention on each self-segment with a desire to learn, grow, and accept whatever it is revealing.

The first key to understanding your feelings is to acknowledge them. As simple as this sounds, many times we fail to acknowledge and accept our feelings because our conditioned mind fears that these feelings are not spiritual, or that we will lose love if we acknowledge them.

Acknowledging our feelings doesn't mean dumping them on everyone else. Often it is advisable to "process" before speaking. This way, you can formulate your responses in a manner that adequately and positively communicates the current state you are experiencing.

As shown in chapter 28, "A Guide to the Emotions," feelings and emotions can be grouped into two basic areas:

1. Feelings that reflect an acceptance of love
2. Feelings that reflect a fear of losing love

Practice identifying what you are feeling and work toward uncovering the deeper elements beneath those feelings. For example, underneath the emotion of anger, one will usually find pain and hurt. You can follow the trail of the initial emotion to the root feeling that exists in the core of your heart.

Key Three: Understanding Your Thought Patterns

Thoughts have been said to be things. This means that what we hold as thought in the mental energies eventually influences our physical actions, which then affect the material forms and substances within our world.

Understanding your thought patterns is perhaps one of the hardest of the seven keys to uncover and understand. This is primarily because we must use thought processes to attempt to understand the thought process itself and the patterns it creates.

One method of understanding our thought patterns is to look at our life's situations and conditions. To some degree, our thought patterns have created our conditions. Of course, there are many other factors that also affect our living conditions. The most important external factor is how other beings' thought patterns and their resultant physical actions influence our lives. While understanding how the thought patterns of others have had an impact on us is important, we need to specifically focus on our own thought patterns. We will find that by modifying our own thought patterns, our actions begin to change and, in consequence, the world around us reacts to this shift in our personal energies and begins to change as well.

Another method of understanding your thought patterns is to ask the thought processor itself (your mind) a question and wait for the answer. Thought processes love to "talk" internally. For example, first ask yourself "why did I have that thought?" or "why did I take that action?"—or other questions phrased in such a way as to elicit a constructive response—then wait for an answer. You will find that you will quickly receive a "thought process" reply.

Sometimes the reply will be complete; other times you will need to ask more questions. As Christ has said, "Ask and ye shall receive," so too can you apply His statements to your own being. Ask of yourself and accept the answers you receive—not as absolute truth, but as ever-deepening clues to uncovering the mysteries of your complete self.

Key Four: Understanding Your Body

Our bodies, as physical matter, are forms and substances existing in the material worlds. As forms and substances they are extensions of thought and thought patterns. As such, our bodies have been projected into the world via creative thought energies in order to experience and gain wisdom. We respect the temple of our body for the ability it gives us to experience the joys of life as well as the sorrows—to learn, appreciate, and grow.

Listening to our bodies can also help us in our basic health concerns. For example, some people have allergic reactions to different foods. In other less virulent but nonetheless real ways, foods and other substances affect our ability to concentrate and approach life in a positive manner. As we pay attention to our bodies, we learn how different substances affect us personally. We can then choose to use or avoid those substances in order to create, enhance, or avoid a specific state of being.

One way to better understand your body is to temporarily limit your functioning. For example, try to not use your hands for a half-hour period. Afterward, write down your thoughts and feelings about what you experienced. Chapter 25 gives some specific suggestions in this area that you may try. As you learn to appreciate your body's abilities, you will come to view your body not as a limitation, but as a valuable asset with which to experience the earth world.

Key Five: Understanding Your Desires

Desire has been said to be the source of all pain, yet when we come to honor our desires and understand them as a component of self-knowledge, we find that they are one of most useful guideposts to zeroing in on our core issues.

Desires come as strong and powerful feelings that create within us an adrenaline-like energy that moves us to action. At times we fear our desires because we have previously acted upon them and experienced some sort of pain as a result. Hence, the statement that "desire is the source of all pain" has been handed down through the ages.

But if we view our desires with a desire to understand them (i.e., why we have them in the first place) then the component energies of the desire separate into discrete parts. Seeing the individual parts of the desire helps us to better understand ourselves. The component parts of desires are thought patterns and feelings. The purpose of these combinations is to create a desired state of being (i.e., happiness, contentment). This can be achieved through internal change or changes in the external world around us.

Your desires are powerful clues to the secrets of your inner self. The next time you want something, take a moment to locate where that particular desire emanates from in your body. Consider how that energy center vibrates when you feel that desire. For example, is the desire coming from your throat center? Perhaps there is a need for you to speak your truth. Next, imagine the desire has been fulfilled. What do you "see" as a result of your desire being fulfilled? Are there any surprises? How do you feel and what are your thoughts?

Key Six: Understanding Your Shadow Self

The shadow self is said to be "part of the light that became darkness" in order to teach. The shadow self is the part of us that fears rejection and craves acceptance. It is the part of us that moves us to act in "negative" patterns in order to test other people's love for us. It is also known as our inner child.

As we begin to nurture and show unconditional love and acceptance toward our inner child, a healing connection between our basic self and our conscious self is forged. This relationship can blossom, encouraging the basic self to share the meaning of its innermost feelings with the other self-segments.

To understand the shadow self, pretend that you are five years old again. You have accidentally broken your mother's crystal vase that was a gift to her from her grandmother. Afraid of losing her favor, you hide the broken pieces of glass in a corner of your bedroom closet (as if your mother will not notice the missing antique or the water spilled on the floor that you did not finish cleaning up). What is it that you want your mother to say to you when she finds the broken glass? What do you want to say to your mother?

Your shadow self is like the five year old child. It needs care and understanding in order to be able to grow and unite with the other parts of the self. You, as the conscious self, must strive to understand and accept the shadow self. Listen to it and nurture it in order to gain a greater integration of all of your self-segments. This will help to align the inner bodies, which will in turn provide the power (the ability) to define, manifest, and complete your life's mission.

Key Seven: Understanding Your Mortality

Life and death are intertwined to such a degree that if we could come to understand our mortality (death), we would then come to understand the mystery of life itself. One by one we will lose everything and everyone that has ever been important to us in our lifetime. Life is a process of first giving meaning to everything and developing relationships between everyone, and then learning to say good-bye to everything and everyone. When we reflect on this reality, every moment of life becomes sacred because all we have is the moment—in every person, element of nature, and creation.

Since no objective proof has yet been made to support life after death, we must come to decide for ourselves what we will choose to believe. This puts the decision to accept or reject God (the afterlife), squarely on our shoulders. By understanding and contemplating our mortality, we are forced to use the attributes of faith and belief to determine for ourselves if death will lead to eternal life, or if it is to be the final experience of our individual consciousness.

By contemplating our mortality we are motivated to live, in the here and now. We are energized to choose and accomplish our life's purpose. We come to cherish the time we have on earth when we fully understand that our bodies will cease to function and we accept the reality of our mortality. The time to live is now, while we are here and in full consciousness.

The Integrated Individual: The Enlightened One

Enlightenment. That elusive state spoken of and written about by sages and mystics and masters for centuries is now unmasked for you to view. It is not a mysterious set of arcane rules and assumptions. Nor is it a secret inner teaching requiring initiations and rituals. Enlightenment does not require you to live a life of asceticism—a life denying yourself the things of this world.

Enlightenment is simply accepting and working with all the segments of the self to live a life rooted in truth, acceptance, and learning. If we do this it becomes only a matter of time before we reach the state of enlightenment, for we are living once again as the ancients prescribed when they said to us: "Man know thyself."

An integrated individual accepts each element of himself or herself as they are, here and now, while always moving toward the soul's purpose. In other words, we do not wait on the sidelines for ourselves to become magically integrated. We participate in our lives. If we do not feel that we can participate, then we can ask for the assistance of the Archangels to give us the inspiration to begin the integration process.

We integrate the five self-segments by first coming to understand them intellectually, and then by learning to experience them in full awareness daily. We literally become a light unto ourselves and shine with a love that knows no end.

Understanding the five segments of the self and their interplay is important in the process of angelic enlightenment. We can better understand these segments by practicing exercises that help us to focus on each self-segment. The two short exercises on the following pages are intended to give you a more direct and conscious awareness of each self-segment and its purpose.

E X E R C I S E

Connecting the Conscious Self to the Soul Self and the Higher Self

Sit quietly in a room by yourself. Make sure that you will not be disturbed for several minutes. Now relax and take a few cleansing breaths. Next, start a countdown in your head beginning at the number seven and moving downward to the number one. Begin counting.

At each number pause and focus your attention as follows:

7 . . . Focus your attention at the base of the spine. Do this gently. Relax the energy there. Wait until it feels balanced. Release any restrictive energy bands that you detect.

6 . . . Focus on the lower abdomen. Once again feel the energy there. Imagine the energy loosening up. Release any restrictive energy bands that you detect.

5 . . . Focus on the area three inches above your navel. See the energy swirl unrestricted and free. Release any restrictive energy bands that you detect.

4 . . . Focus on the heart area. Feel the energy warm and soothe you. Release any restrictive energy bands that you detect.

3 . . . Focus on the throat area. Relax the throat area. Allow the energy to flow. Release any restrictive energy bands that you detect.

2 . . . Focus on the area between your eyebrows called the third eye. Imagine that the energy is spinning freely. Release any energy bands that you detect.

1 . . . Focus on the top of your head. Open to the energy of the universe. Release any restrictive energy bands that you detect.

Now imagine that circular bands are breaking apart all around you—from the base of your spine to the top of your head. They release and fall to the ground. Your energy is now flowing, natural and free. Energy from within you moves outward like circular waves on a pond in multiple layers.

As the energy rings move outward you begin to float upward, gently upward. Allow yourself to be. Float on this stream of positive energy. You swirl within its light and you can feel its gentle power. After a short time you find yourself encompassed in light. From this vantage point you can see, know, and be in all directions simultaneously! This is the view of the soul self.

Off to the side you see the higher self. It appears to be a pool of wisdom shimmering beside you. Golden pearls of wisdom float on its sapphire surface. Each pearl is gleaming from the light reflected on it from all around you.

Down below you, you see the energy stream that leads to the earth world and the body that your conscious self resides in. You send loving currents down the energy stream as well as messages of support and direction.

You pick up a wisdom pearl from the pool of the higher self and place it into the energy stream. It dissolves into drops of golden liquid as it travels down the energy stream to the conscious self.

You reside in this state for a few minutes while marveling at the light, awareness, and contentment that you are experiencing. When you are finished, relax and gently allow your awareness to descend to the body and the earth. After a few seconds open your eyes. Take a deep breath and move your body. Take some time to review and integrate your experience. You may want to write it down as well.

E X E R C I S E

Connecting the Conscious Self with the Emotional and Basic Self

Sit down in an easy chair or lie on a bed. Allow yourself to relax. Feel the tension in your body melt away. After a while you become aware of something tugging at your conscience. In your heart, back somewhere inside you, you feel an insistence. Imagine that you turn around to face the source of this insistence. You begin to walk.

It is dark and you are holding onto a rail on the side of a wall or tunnel. Move along the walkway while holding onto the rail. You walk for awhile, unsure of where you are going. You feel the tugging gently continuing. After a short time you see a dim light up ahead. You move toward the light as you continue to hold onto the rail for support.

You move closer and see a closed door. You come to the door and stop. On the door is a wooden knocker in the shape of a lion's head. You move your hand to the knocker and knock three times. After a few moments, the door slowly opens to a scene. This is a scene from the past, from your life. This scene is shown to you by your emotional self. It can be one of unresolved hurt and regret or one of joy and happiness. Walk into the room quietly and just be.

As you watch the scene, you begin to feel a presence from behind you. It is urging you to take action and to do something. This is your basic self. Follow its urging and join the scene that the emotional self has presented. Become a part of the scene and interact with its contents and personalities. Do this for a few minutes—as long as it seems comfortable.

After awhile, when it feels right, bid the scene farewell. Embrace the basic self and the emotional self and thank them for their assistance. Then leave the room and close the door with the lion's head knocker behind you.

The way back is easier, as you follow the light of the conscious self back to waking awareness. Open your eyes and rest for a moment. Ponder the meaning of this experience. This has been a message from your emotional and basic selves.

Try these two exercises. Give yourself room to experience them. As you continue toward angelic enlightenment, remember that all segments of the self become integrated. We are not any single segment, but all segments at the same time. This is our humanity and in truth we are of one energy—the energy of the Creator.

Dreams are often your basic self's way of resolving
the inconsistencies of waking life—the concerns you do not
choose to face consciously.

4

Experiences and the Spiritual Toolkit of Angelic Enlightenment

THE TECHNIQUES AND methodologies of angelic enlightenment include, but are not limited to, the five basic types highlighted in this chapter. They are: prayer; meditation and contemplation; dream interpretation; past life recall; and sound, music, and vibration. In addition to these tools, each Archangel has a main technique that is written about in their respective section.

You can think of these methods and techniques as individual tools in your spiritual toolkit. Each tool has a purpose. It helps you complete a task. After that task is complete, the tool is put away for use at a later time when it makes sense to use it again. The tool is not the goal! Nor is simply using the tool at certain intervals, or for a specific length of time, the goal.

Imagine using a screwdriver to tighten a screw in a curtain rod because the rod was loose on the wall. Is using the screwdriver the goal of the experience? Is the goal to use the screwdriver daily? Does the fact that you are simply using the screwdriver make you a better person? Of course the answer to all of these questions is no!

Another analogy about spiritual tools and their purpose is the Thanksgiving Trip analogy. In this example, a man is going to return home to have Thanksgiving dinner with his father, whom he has not seen for many years. As the prodigal son went into the world, only to return, so too has this man now come to the point of desire to see and learn from the past—from his father. He must travel across country for the Thanksgiving holiday.

First, he must decide what method of travel to use to accomplish his goal. He can take a plane or perhaps a train. He can also take a bus or even drive. In this case, he decides to drive.

Next, he must decide which route to follow to get to his father's house. He pulls out his map and comes up with two possible routes. He consults weather reports to decide if he should take the northern route or the southern route and to determine which states he would need to travel through to get to his destination.

Finally he gets into his car and begins his journey. Over the course of three days and after traveling through various states he reaches his goal—his father's house—and partakes of the food that his father has prepared for their meal. Their reunion is a joyous one, marked by acceptance, deep feeling, and love.

In this analogy:

- The man (son) represents ourselves.
- The vehicle (car) that he used to reach his goal represents the spiritual tool we choose to use when opening to divine energy.
- Consulting the map and checking on the current weather report represents honestly viewing our motivations and current life situation as we begin our spiritual journey.
- The states the son traveled through represent the various states of consciousness that we experience on the way to our spiritual goals.
- The father represents our soul self, and the food prepared for the meal represents the wisdom of the higher self.
- The joyousness of the reunion indicates what the experience of soul infusion is like as each of our self-segments comes into alignment with divine energy and with soul's pattern for this lifetime.

We use tools as we need them. They serve their purpose and are then set aside. Living our life consists of simply being. Once the man (son) reached his father's house as described in the story above, he did not stay in his car. It was set aside as he joined his father in Thanksgiving.

The tools of angelic enlightenment help us make adjustments and fine-tune our inner worlds. They help us focus on experiences for processing as well as focusing on the wisdom (processed and integrated experiences) of the higher self. They also help us open ourselves to the energies of the Archangels and other divine beings.

What Are Experiences?

What are experiences? The answer to this question is that experiences are slices of life that carry the vibrational imprint of all levels of our awareness at a specific time. By that definition, we come to see that each and every experience contains the complete mystery of life itself!

Experiences can lead us to particular states of consciousness. By using spiritual tools, we can realign ourselves to the levels of a particular experience, hence achieving its corresponding state of consciousness. Within us is the memory and experience of the heavenly worlds of the Creator. The states of *being* that are associated with the great mystics of the past and present are ours, for we have experienced such states and can experience them again.

We, as souls having a human embodiment, process multiple types of experiences. Soul is constantly teaching us, not just during our waking state, but also during sleep states, dream states, and daydreams. The main types of experiences that we can process using the spiritual toolkit of angelic enlightenment are: present experiences; past experiences; dream experiences; and imaginative experiences (daydreams).

Present Experiences

This is our day-to-day waking life. We strive to process our daily experiences as they occur. By processing our experiences every day, we stop the pattern of piling up more and more unprocessed experiences that will probably require later review. By ignoring what we, in our hearts, know we should be facing and dealing with, we not only add to our own load for the future, but in subtle ways begin to close off to the lifestream in the present. This has less to do with repression than practicality. We cannot process all present experiences simultaneously; many times processing leads to the past and in itself takes physical time. But we can process our day-to-day experiences with self-truth by acknowledging to ourselves that we have issues to face as we feel the many emotions triggered within us during our day. From this point of view, we strive to express our emotions in a healthy way instead of repressing them. A good way to remain current with our day-to-day experiences is to use the L.E.A.R.N. technique discussed in chapter 15, specifically the nightly review segment.

Past Experiences

The past was once the present, as the future shall become the present, and then the past. When we speak of *experience,* we mean a *state of being.* This state of being consists of the exact mental, emotional, spiritual, physical, and subconscious alignments of divine energy existing in a moment of time.

Unprocessed experiences lie waiting for us to uncover and examine. When we are perplexed in the present, or when we begin to consciously process our present life, our attention is very often directed to past experiences. When we are confused by the emotions in the present and do not know why we are feeling as we do, it is time to explore the past for an answer.

We strive to process our experiences from the past. This past can be yesterday or twenty years ago. As we work on examining our responses in the present, we are inevitably drawn to the past to seek the root experience. This is where the trail we follow leads us for understanding and growth. So, in a way, processing the past is processing the present since we are always here, always now. By delving into our past we can heal old scars on our hearts, deal with any regrets we may have, and embrace our experience in a way that we may have been unable to when the experience first occurred.

Experiences from the past can include past lifetimes. The knowledge from these past lifetimes can be accessed and used in the present to help us return to states of consciousness where we wish to reside, but have forgotten how to achieve. These experiences are stored inside the repository called the higher self.

Dream Experiences

At first it may appear strange to view dreams as experiences of life, but that is what they are! As messages from the soul self or the basic self, they are experiences that we process through the techniques of dream interpretation. Dream experiences are sometimes incredible and fantastic. In dreams, we have experiences that we cannot have in physical life, such as flying dreams.

Dreams are also the subconscious mind's way of blowing off steam. Unresolved issues from the life of the dreamer come up in ways that are often perplexing. In addition, each dreamer's symbology is different from another's. In chapter 27, you will learn how to understand and uncover your dream symbology.

Imaginative Experiences (Daydreams)

One of the most relaxing and precious experiences is found in the daytime wanderings of our inner self. In daydreams, we have experiences fashioned by the what-if principle. Other times we move to past states of awareness in what is known as reverie. This time is important for us. To remember the past and use the wisdom gained there is to enliven the present with the full sum of our spiritual self.

Spiritual Tools Help Us Process Our Experiences

We use prayer, past life recall, meditation, contemplation, sound and music, and dream interpretation as methods to achieve a state of focus that enables us to gain access to the higher self. This opens us to the knowledge and direction of the soul self. Once opened to these sources and operating from the spirit of self-truth and honesty, we can clearly work through our experience and integrate its lessons.

Prayer

Prayer is a way for us to reach into our hearts to ask for the assistance of God's divine power and grace. We do not see prayer as a way to get things that we want, nor as a way to enforce our will upon others. Prayer is a way to communicate with the sacred part of ourselves.

The wording of a prayer is important, as important as the intentions behind it. The prayers in this book, inspired by the Angels, promote self-empowerment. Prayers that ask for assistance and guidance in integrating the self are addressed to the individual Archangel as appropriate.

By reviewing what we ask for in our prayers, we can learn more about what we are feeling regarding a particular situation or person in our lives. The following is an example of a prayer request followed by that same request expressed in a way that more fully describes our inner concerns. As we pray, we can try to continually reach deeper into our own hearts to clearly communicate to ourselves and to our Creator who we are and what we are feeling.

Prayer Example 1: "Dear Lord, please help my son to stop acting irresponsibly and make him stop drinking."

Prayer Example 2: "Dear Lord, please help my son by sending him the strength of your presence so that he may understand why he is unable to control his actions. I pray that he may be able to face his pain and heal his heart. I hope that he can forgive me for the hurt I may have caused him. Please protect him through this difficult time."

The following prayer is addressed to one of the Archangels. You can use the prayers in this book as appropriate or modify them as you need to:

Dear Archangel Michael,

I pray to you so that I may strengthen my awareness of your divine inspiration in my life. I open my heart to you and ask you to bestow upon me your divine energy. I ask that you help me to remove the masks from my heart and to live in the spirit of Truth, Honesty, and Justice more and more each day.

I ask this of you through the universal Christ energy, Amen.

Prayer is a way of talking with your inner self to uncover your desires. Desires are the source of growth. As you allow your inner desires to surface, try to view them with an open mind and follow them to their root source. With prayer, we focus on the experiences of our life with a desire to improve and to grow. We desire this growth for ourselves, our loved ones, and mankind itself. The Creator does not need our prayers. We do. Prayers can lead us to uncovering more of our divine nature.

Dream Interpretations

Dreams are used in the angelic enlightenment process primarily for their power as symbolic messages from one or more of the self-segments via the higher self. By learning the language of dreams we can effectively interpret these sleep messages. Issues that were in the background or issues that we are confused about are brought to our attention for greater understanding. The result is that we focus on issues that are important for us to resolve in order to keep attuned to our soul's purpose or to maintain emotional balance. We may receive guidance in a dream as to a particular course of action to take in a given situation or relationship.

Proper understanding of a dream's symbols is important, and we must be careful not to rationalize the meaning of our dreams so that they fit the self-protective mechanisms of a non-integrated basic self, or any of the selves that are in denial and repression. In other words, we must be watchful to not allow the conscious mind to ignore the true message from the dream self (chapter 27 discusses understanding dream symbols).

Occasionally, we can have dream experiences with beings of the Angelic realms beyond this earth world. These dreams are often marked by their clarity and vividness. Compared to these highly lucid dreams, other dreams may appear two-dimensional.

At this point, it is good to remember that the purpose of garnering the Angels' assistance is to learn to stand on our own spiritual feet. We attain this, in part, by clearing the blocks to our own humanity. Like a father and mother help their child to grow and become self-sufficient, so too do the Angelic beings look after us.

When you call upon the angels for help, they lend their assistance in the form best suited for our learning and growth. A good parent knows when to step in and help their child, and when to stand back to let the child try for themselves. The Angels do the same.

Everybody dreams. You may not recall your dreams, but you do dream. Dreams are necessary to our physical, emotional, mental, and spiritual well-being. Studies show that subjects who are repeatedly awakened when just entering the REM sleep cycle often exhibit disturbing symptoms. These symptoms include weight loss, irritability, confusion, and in extreme cases the inability to function day-to-day. Proper dream interpretation extends the built-in physio-spiritual function of dreaming so that we can learn as much as we can from the dream experience.

Meditation and Contemplation

Meditation involves the temporary stilling of the mind. By focusing the conscious/intellectual self on a particular image, mantra, or area of the body, for example, the normal waking thought stream is set aside and we can become aware of other thought streams. Usually filled with the wisdom from the higher self or messages from our soul self, these thought streams can be experienced in a multi-dimensional environment as your body sits in a calm state of detachment from the sensory world.

Breathing and chanting exercises are often a part of meditative techniques. These exercises assist with the meditative experience by entraining the physical body systems and brain to deeper patterns of relaxation, which in turn allows us to become aware of the other energy centers. These energy centers are normally far too quiet to recognize amid the relative noise of our day-to-day interactions with the workaday world.

Contemplation, which is akin to meditation, is similar to using the imagination such as in creative visualization. In contemplation, one may take a confusing situation or perplexing dream and view it from many different angles. This virtual psychic domain we each possess is a powerful inner laboratory. In it we can experiment to our heart's content with concepts and patterns in order to come to a deeper understanding of our life's experiences.

Guided meditation can help you to re-connect with the various energy centers of your etheric body in order to regulate their energy flow. There are seven major energy centers in the etheric body. They are also known as chakras. The seven energy centers and their location, color, and purpose are shown in the chart below.

Number	Name	Location	Color	Purpose
Seventh	Crown	top of head	purple/white	brings in the spiritual God energy
Sixth	Third Eye	forehead between eyebrows	indigo (bluish-purple)	clarity in seeing; precognition
Fifth	Throat	throat	blue	truth in speaking and hearing; clairaudience
Fourth	Heart	heart	green	love, growth, and caring
Third	Solar Plexus (three inches above navel)	solar plexus	yellow	emotions, feeling, sensing
Second	Sexual	genitals	orange	reproduction, creativity
First	Base	base of spine	deep red	instincts, physical health, connection with earth energy

The Seven Chakras

You can use guided meditation to explore the energy centers. You may be drawn to areas or centers that feel blocked. Use your imagination to feel the energy coming into balance or opening up in that particular area. The energy centers are receptive to your thoughts and imaging. For example, when trying to revitalize a center, imagine breathing in energy in the color related to the specific center (i.e., breathe in indigo for the third eye center).

During this process you may become aware of hidden issues. Deal with these issues. They are probably related to the energy center you are currently focusing on. They are part of the root issues that may have caused an imbalance in a particular center. Acknowledge them, feel them, and resolve them if needed or desired—either during the meditation or later.

Past Life Recall and Regression

Past life recall is also used to integrate the self-segments. By becoming aware of past life experiences through contact with the higher self, we bring into play the lessons learned in the past. We are each, of course, a composite of all of our experiences. When we cannot seem to find an answer to a problem within our current life experiences, awareness from the past may hold the key to action in the present. Some people may recall past lives while others may not. Recall can come in dreams or through direct psychic experience, either visually or intuitively. Past life readings and regressions, as well as self-administered techniques, can help you to access the wisdom from the higher self.

A short discussion of karma, and how we view karma, is appropriate here. We believe that we are soul, and that soul sends down into matter (earth life) a part of itself, our personality, in order to experience, learn, grow, and evolve. We believe that we choose, as soul, what we want to experience in each lifetime. This involves our choice as to what of our former cause and effect, or karma, we want to wholly integrate in order to complete that cycle of experience.

In our opinion, karma is not a punishment for past wrongdoings; rather it represents how much we want to try to tackle, or learn from, in one lifetime. We each have free will to choose the learning experiences we will have in each life. The skills and abilities developed in past lifetimes can be tapped into and applied in new ways in each lifetime. But when karma is used by others—perhaps by some spiritual paths—to control our actions, we will find ourselves limited. We may block our ability to resolve the issues in our life. The L.E.A.R.N. technique will outline the problems that can come from rationalizing experiences to fit a particular belief system.

Remember that past life experiences are no different than current life experiences. They are complete vibrational slices or pictures in time. Often during a past life regression, issues will be sent to the conscious self from the higher self through the initiative of the soul self. In this way, the experiences and the wisdom of the past life can be accessed by you in the present.

The concern with any experience is that we fail to learn from it. The moment now always becomes the past. As quickly as we experience, we move to the next experience. Do not forget to live in the moment even as you process the past.

Sound, Music, and Vibration

Sound and music also play an important role in the attainment of angelic enlightenment. Sound and music act mainly upon the physical and emotional centers. But since the self-segments are interconnected, we find that when one is acted on, all other self-segments are affected as well.

Sound and music can be used to entrain the physical brain to specific wave frequencies. It has been documented that certain brain wave frequencies are conducive to out-of-the-body projection, dream travel, ESP, prophecy, general healing, and well-being. Chanting is a well-known technique using sound for spiritual expansion. Through the warbling and wavering effect of chanting, sound reaches the brain through the left ear and right ear at a slightly different frequency. This difference becomes the frequency that the brain entrains to.

Music, known as the universal language of soul, communicates without words in a mysterious way that few other languages can come close to doing. As you integrate your self-segments, you may have the experience of spontaneously singing to yourself out loud. You will find that various styles of music will resonate within you, bringing forth issues that you need to view and work with.

For example, music with a heavy beat may help you get in touch with your basic self and its issues. At other times, this kind of music will help you to get in touch with your anger over past events. Various musical styles can be used to stimulate different parts of the self.

They're Playing our Song

Music has the power to transport us in time to specific states of being that carry their own vibrational imprint. How many times have you heard a song on the radio and been transported back to the time frame of the song? The song not only moves your focus to a different time, but also brings up various emotions connected to experiences from that time. In this way, you can use music to realign your current self to a state of consciousness that you wish or need to experience again.

Try to use the power of music to take you to the state of awareness that you wish to reside in. From there you can explore how you came into that experience or state to begin with. You may learn more than you expect to. In some cases, you can even heal yourself by aligning yourself to a state where divine energy was flowing through you, unimpeded by restrictions of your own making.

How Chanting and Vibration Help You

Chanting has been used for centuries as a tool for focusing on higher powers. It is not the words themselves that provide the greatest benefit of chanting; rather, it is how it affects the brain. Chanting creates vibrational changes to the physical body/brain mechanism. Closing your eyes certainly changes the way you feel. You can no longer see what is around you and your focus moves to the feeling (tactile) and hearing (auditory) centers of your brain function.

When you chant a word or mantra, the sound vibrations that emanate from your voice are transferred to your brain in slightly different frequencies as a result of the positions of the ears and the variations in tone of the singing or chanting. Just as a Tibetan singing bowl creates sounds of varying frequencies, chanting sets in motion a sound with a warbling effect. The left ear and right ear hear different frequencies of the sound. The frequencies are very close together and it is the difference in the frequencies as they are processed by the brain that entrains the brain to that specific frequency.

Studies on brain waves have found several groups or levels of brain wave activity known in summary as: Beta, Alpha, Theta, and Delta. Each of these groups have an associated frequency such as 6 Hz. Simply speaking, when the left brain processes the sound from the right ear at 12000 Hz and the right brain processes the sound from the left ear at 12010 Hz then the brain is entrained at 10 Hz.

Wave Type	Frequency Range	Description
Beta	13–30 Hz	Externally Directed Attention (alert)
Alpha	8–13 Hz	Relaxation State
Theta	4–7 Hz	Deep Reverie, access to deep memories
Delta	0.5–4 Hz	Deep Sleep

Brain wave activity and sound frequencies

Chanting, kept up long enough, causes a real physical change in brain wave patterns. This affects the way you feel, your ability to visualize, and can allow you to tap into unused centers of the brain. Are these centers the building blocks of dreams or portals into the heavenly worlds?

In any case, the use of chanting and vibration helps us to calm the body and brain in order to access information from divine sources. This information helps us to process the experiences we are concerned with in the immediate present.

The End Result: Allowing Ourselves to Be

Life is an ongoing process. We learn through the Sword of Truth how to honestly view our reactions to the experiences of life. Then we express our feelings, accept our experience, and release the cycle of learning for integration into the higher self. We then ask ourselves how we can act differently in future situations. We have taken the knowledge gained and applied it in our lives.

What we are after is not the ability to use the spiritual tools or the ability to simply act. What we are after is keeping our hearts open to the spirit of life and living in a state of love and bliss. The end result of angelic enlightenment is represented by the Archangel Uriel: to simply be.

Detachment is accepting the reality of your life
as it is in this very moment.

5

Starting Your Journey with the Archangels

THE FOUR ARCHANGELS are prepared to take you on a journey. This chapter discusses how you can prepare for that journey. It tells you what you'll need to take with you and what you'll need to leave behind. It will talk about how long the journey is and what you can expect to see when you get there. Finally, it will give you the next step you need to start the journey for yourself.

What to Take on Your Journey: Desire

When viewed closely, desire—in particular our own desires—are but a trail to an understanding and acceptance of our complete self, as both a student of spirituality and of humanity. These two studies, spirituality and humanity, cannot be split apart, and one cannot be learned at the expense of the other. The person who marries these two studies into one overall exploration of life will engender within himself a compassion and love for mankind and a desire to discover the secrets of life and death, of God and Spirit, in such a way as to benefit all around him.

When we begin to focus upon ourselves, our experiences, and our feelings, and live day-to-day while accepting our humanity, the spiritual elements that we seek are found to be beside us all along. Your spiritual mission will become clear and you will follow it and live it. By processing your feelings daily, you allow the heart to remain in its natural state of openness and love. This is an experience of the grace of God.

The overwhelming spirit of life now moves our voice, our hands, our hearts. Every movement is done in the peace and harmony of this spirit. Yet there are times when we unconsciously impede this flow of love, in much the same way a dam impedes the flow of a river. The water backs up. Eventually the dam will burst and the love we withheld will, of necessity, flow out through us into the world.

By honestly processing our day-to-day experiences, we can keep the dam from forming in the first place. This will help us to avoid the ups and downs of giving love, withholding love, giving love, and withholding love over and over again, never understanding the forces that push and pull us into this up and down cycle.

In order to achieve self-mastery (self-knowledge), we should first strive to accept who we are, the feelings we feel, and the desires we have. Secondly, we should strive to understand why we desire what we do while simultaneously not condemning ourselves. By following the trail of our desires, we begin our journey of self-discovery. This journey is in essence what the ancients first prescribed: "Man know thyself." Now that is not: Man *change* thyself, or Man *condemn* thyself, or even Man *live by a set of laws*. It is simply: "Man *know* thyself."

What to Leave Behind on Your Journey: Self-Limiting Beliefs

Self-limiting beliefs are beliefs that limit your power. Power is defined in the positive as the ability to act. This ability to act is crucial, for we are in a world that requires creation to transmute the divine energy into various forms for achieving goals within the realms of matter, energy, space, and time.

By the incorrect analysis and application of the lessons of an experience, we can unwittingly install limiting beliefs that change our destiny. Our destiny has been said to be our destination. By changing our beliefs, we change our experiences. And by changing our experiences, we change our destiny or our final destination.

The Archangels' plan will teach you how to create new patterns that help you to remove self-limiting beliefs. You can then empower yourself with positive beliefs that help you live the kind of life that you truly desire.

Power and desire have taken on negative connotations through many paths and teachings. It is not power and desire that are negative, but rather the misapplication of these concepts. Once we extend these concepts outside of our own personal space in an effort to use our power to act upon other people or aim our desires at changing another against their will, we cross the line between creativity and destruction. Proper application of the principles of power and of desire is essential in fulfilling our life's mission and in living a life according to soul's pattern and the divine plan.

Self-limiting beliefs should be left unpacked as you begin your journey. If you take some along by accident, don't worry. There are many places along the way where you can discard unwanted patterns as you learn why you came to accept them in the first place!

How Long Will the Journey Take?

The pace and length of the journey will vary from individual to individual. Each of us is a unique being with varied experiences in this life and in the past. If you are sincere and commit to the process of angelic enlightenment, you will find that the process moves as the seasons move—slowly, but surely.

The four Archangels work together to assist you—at times independent of each other and at times concurrently. The time spent with Archangel Michael can vary depending upon the amount of repression that has bound your life in discordance.

Sometime after Michael has begun to assist you, the Archangel Raphael will come to help you deal with the truths you are now allowing yourself to unseal and view. The length of time spent with Raphael will depend on the amount of pain that you have left unprocessed from the past and how willing you are to process that pain now.

After accepting the truth of your choices and healing the wounds of your heart, you are in a position to accept the challenge of defining and carrying out the steps to accomplish your life's mission. The Archangel Gabriel comes to you to offer you the divine dispatch—to take the initiative to fulfill the soul's purpose for this lifetime. This involves defining that purpose and making concrete plans and guidelines for achieving that purpose.

Gabriel will teach you about the divine energy of creation, maintenance, and dissolution. You will work along with the patterns of nature and be required to develop the strength to continue the process of angelic enlightenment through to completion. The amount of time in this area of development depends on your particular mission and situation.

Uriel comes to help you find appreciation in simply living. Through the guidance of the other Archangels, you have become the integrated human being. You are one whose inner bodies are in harmony with the outer world. The energy from the Holy Spirit comes to you through the soul self unimpeded by unconscious patterns of limitation. The time spent with the Archangel Uriel is dependent on your progress in processing your experiences and integrating their wisdom while working along with Michael, Raphael, and Gabriel.

There are no hard and fast timelines for enlightenment. We end up using what we will learn during the journey to angelic enlightenment forever—the Archangels Michael, Raphael, Gabriel, and Uriel will be here for us always. The lessons we have learned become integrated into our higher self. We have cleared the blockages in our energy centers. This allows progressively greater amounts of divine energy to enter into our hearts and flow out to the world.

What You Can Expect to See at Your Journey's End

Can you imagine the limitless love of the Creator moving through you continually? Do you want to experience unending bliss and deep insight into nature, yourself, and others? Can you remember living "in tune with the infinite?" Can you imagine being as the little child? How would it feel to have your heart full and overflowing with love, compassion, and joy?

This and more awaits you at your journey's end—this and the pains and sorrows of human life. You see, we do not give up our humanity to gain angelic enlightenment. Rather, we embrace it and all that goes with it. The pain, the pleasure, the agony, and the ecstasy. Through an acceptance of life as it is, with the desire to love and to bring more love into the world, we live our lives in sync with spirit and soul's pattern. We find that each step we take and each word we speak is filled with the power and purpose of the Holy Spirit.

Your Future, Our Future, The Future

Our future is entirely predictable if we can learn to see and interpret the patterns of our own being. By using the spiritual toolkit, you can become more aware of your patterns and the ways you have learned to respond to and process your experiences.

Once you clearly see the patterns that drive your life, the future loses its mysterious hold on you. By applying what you are learning you begin to realize that the future is, in essence, the experiences that will come to you as a result of the choices that you consciously make in the present. These choices may end in success or in failure.

No one knows the heights to which we may rise and the depths that our insights into ourselves and life can penetrate. Therefore, no one yet knows the complete future. Therein lies a great adventure, open to all who have been given the gift of consciousness. Take the gift of life and construct a future that you wish to reside in!

Your Next Step is the First Step Toward Enlightenment

Pack your bags, you are ready to start your journey. In the next section of the book you will meet the Archangel Michael. Michael is the Archangel of truth and justice. He will help you to view the truth of your actions and choices. Follow his guidance. This is your first step toward angelic enlightenment.

To help as you work with Michael, be sure to try the Charting Your Life exercise (chapter 10) inspired by him. Use the meditations and prayers as outlined in section two. Pay close attention to your dreams and take some time to review them. Learn to understand the messages from your inner worlds.

Be easy on yourself. This is not a journey of self-condemnation, but one of self-acceptance and renewal. You are loved—and you are a loving being. May your journey be filled with adventure, growth, and understanding.

The spiritual need is a human need.

Section 2

The Archangel Michael

An angel can illume the thought and mind of man
by strengthening the power of vision,
and by bringing within his reach
some truth which the angel himself contemplates.

—St. Thomas Aquinas, *The Bliss of the Way*

6

Michael: The Archangel of Truth and Justice

THE FIRST ARCHANGEL to guide you on your journey is Saint Michael. Michael is normally pictured in armor with a sword in his right hand and a scale in his left hand. He is sometimes pictured in battle with his heel on the nape of a fallen Angel's neck. This symbolizes the ultimate illumination of the higher self over the egocentric self.

It was the Archangel Michael who first made his presence known to Peter as Peter began his cycle of exploration into the Angelic realms. It was with the help and assistance of Michael's energy that Peter began to break out of his self-created barriers. He was then able to participate in the truth of his life from a position of alignment with his soul's pattern and purpose.

With the help of Michael, we find that truth is the state of understanding ourselves. We achieve this state by objectively viewing the patterns of our conditioning. This helps us to see the truth of how the conscious self (the personality) makes decisions. By accepting the truth of our conditioning, we empower ourselves to change the reality that we experience by changing our own patterns.

The attribute of justice can be viewed as a willingness to accept the cycle of experience that our choices have brought to us. This relates to the concept of karma and cause and effect. The attribute of justice is self-focused. In other words, we do not seek to enforce justice on others. Self-reflective justice is the type of justice that Michael represents within angelic enlightenment.

The attribute of honesty applies to both self-honesty and honesty to those around us. One aspect of being honest is that we do not misrepresent (to ourselves or others) the patterns of our conditioning that we have come to understand.

For example, let's say that someone comes to accept the truth that they may have a pattern that influences them to shoplift. It would be dishonest for them to tell themselves that they do not have a problem or inclination to shoplift. It would also be dishonest for them to misrepresent themselves to others as a person to be trusted alone in a store. By being honest, we give ourselves space to be. This gives us the room to view ways to change our patterns and to seek the deeper reasons why they exist in the first place. Truth is essential. If we do not admit to having a problem, then there is no way we can correct or change the unconscious patterns that surround and provoke the problem.

There comes a time for each of us when we are given the challenge to face the issues in life that require us to honestly deal with our choices as they have manifested in our lives. This time is marked by our awareness of the Sword of Truth of the Archangel Michael.

This symbolic sword, The Sword of Truth, is wielded by those courageous individuals who accept the conscious task of integrating their lives by processing their past and current experiences in order to live a more full, loving, and passionate life. Each of us has this Sword of Truth at our disposal at this very moment. It sits in its sheath awaiting our command. With it we can cut through internal barriers that are keeping us from accomplishing our life's purpose, the attainment of self-knowledge, and the integration of our self-segments.

The Three Attributes of the Sword of Truth

1. **Realization.** Realizing that you, at this very moment, carry the Sword of Truth with you at all times. There are no formulas, nor man-made masters, that must be purchased. All you need is in you now.

2. **Courage.** Generating the courage to lift the Sword from the sheath at your side and using it to understand yourself and your purpose. You may be surprised by what you see.

3. **Commitment.** Commitment means that once you wield the Sword
   of Truth there is no turning back. One must comply with the honesty
   that is required when the Sword of Truth is unsheathed. One must move
   forward in commitment, at all times striving to see the truth of one's actions
   and desires.

It is quite probable that since you are now reading this information, you have
already used the Sword of Truth, or are about to be presented with possibly the
greatest challenge of your life—one that you have been waiting for—for all of your
life. To become a bearer of The Sword of Truth.

Belief Does Not Equal Truth

Belief does not equal truth, yet belief affects the experiences you have in your life. For
example, if you believe you are not proficient in a particular sport, and you equate
poor performance with pain, you will not choose to play that particular sport. This
limits your experience. This also prevents any experiences that would come from
playing that sport, both positive and negative. Conversely, if you believe that with
enough practice you can become proficient in anything, then you are more likely to
try learning new things. This belief affects your experiences as well.

Consider that you are standing on a beach. You are facing away from the water
toward the land. In front of you is a forest and behind you is the ocean. You start
walking. Your experience will be vastly different depending on the direction you are
facing as you start to walk. If facing the forest, you will likely enter the forest and see
the trees and the forest animals. If you are facing the ocean, you will experience the
sand, water, waves, and sea life. In a similar way, our beliefs focus the scope of our
available experiences into a particular vibrational bandwidth. They define our field
of view; our viewpoints. Since we are locked into a set of viewpoints based on our
belief system, we can only experience life from that set of viewpoints!

As you can see, belief does not equal truth—it equals a particular alignment of
your viewpoint. This alignment either increases or decreases the available experiences that you can encounter. Try extending this physical analogy into your spiritual
belief systems.

Some people consider their set of beliefs to be like keys. They feel that if they hold the proper set of beliefs, then they are in reality holding keys to the Heavenly kingdom. They believe that these keys will provide them salvation in spirit after the death of their body. They believe that if they fail to hold the proper beliefs, they will be unable to unlock the door of Heaven at the time of death.

One of the goals of angelic enlightenment is to help you to gain a greater awareness of your belief systems. By following the guidance of Archangel Michael and practicing the techniques inspired by him you may come to understand why you believe what you do. You may then choose to change your beliefs. Changing your beliefs will change the set of viewpoints that you allow yourself to hold. Changing your set of viewpoints presents you with a different bandwidth of experience.

How Beliefs are Formed

Michael teaches that our beliefs are formed by the processing of our experiences. In processing our experiences, we make assumptions of cause and effect. Over time these become part of our belief systems, which can limit our experiences. The Archangels encourage us to process from a soul-infused state. When we integrate all the self-segments and process from a state of soul-infusion, we are able to extract the full learning potential from each and every experience.

When we touch fire with our hand, we get burned. We process that experience and learn that if we touch the fire we will hurt ourselves. We form the belief that fire will hurt us based on integrating the wisdom from the experience through processing. We come to know how to physically interact with the environment by processing our interactions with the environment.

Beliefs are also formed by our experiences with our relationship contacts. Our parents are usually our primary contacts early in life. As we grow, our contacts expand to include interactions with our siblings, relatives, friends, and the world at large. Patterns of acceptance and rejection that we encounter create beliefs in us.

The beliefs formed by our relationships define a bandwidth of experiences that we can have. Like a serpent eating its own tail, we can figuratively spin within a bandwidth of experience because the bandwidth reflects back onto itself. These patterns can keep our attention focused on specific areas for months and years until another energy from outside of our conscious self acts upon us.

A principle of physics states that an object will remain in motion until another force comes into play upon it. Likewise, your beliefs keep your experiences moving in a certain direction (within a bandwidth) until another force comes into play upon you. This can occur in several ways.

For example, once you make the effort (direct energy) to examine your beliefs—to understand how they were formed and to choose to accept or change them—you introduce a new force upon yourself. Energy can also be directed into your life from external energy sources such as other people, the environment, your other self-segments, and the spiritual realms. These external energy sources act as forces that play upon you. They can influence you to change your beliefs.

Time: False or Real?

Time waits for no one. The world marches on. It has been said in metaphysical terms that time and space are illusions. From the viewpoint of eternity, the concepts of time and space lose some of their significance. But when you live in a world of embodiments, time and space are of critical importance. They have great meaning and are neither an illusion nor a trap to hold you and bind you from truth.

Time itself and the extension of time is an experience. Experiences over time can often generate enough accumulated energy to influence you to modify your beliefs. For example, let's say that you believe a certain meditative technique will bring you peace and bliss. Over a period of months and years, you continue to practice this technique. Your results were far less than expected; your belief that this meditation technique will work for you has been diminished.

Often, people will not fully process their experiences and accept the lessons they present. This is also known as repression. In the meditative technique example, we find that even though the technique did not result in what it promised, the meditator may choose to blame himself. He may tell himself that he did not practice the technique correctly or that he is not spiritually mature enough for it to work. He may have a host of other excuses all pointed at the self.

Pointing blame toward ourselves is sometimes done to protect other interests of the self. For example, if the meditator chooses to change his belief in the meditative technique, he may also be internally pressured to change his belief in the spiritual path or religion that promoted the technique. By acknowledging to himself that the meditative technique did not bring what was promised, he will need to consider that the rest of his path may be out of alignment with his soul's plan and purpose. He may feel the need to change his life. Change is difficult for most of us, especially major life changes. Spiritual path changes are major life changes.

Ask yourself, "What does it profit me to repress the processing of my experiences?" Even if that processing leads you to leave old surroundings, old relationships, and old paths, there is no reason to delay. In the long run you may end up leaving those anyway, worn and weary from years of repression.

Take the time now to be true to yourself. Later, after you have healed the wounds of the past and processed your experiences with the assistance of the Archangel Raphael, the Archangel Gabriel will come to teach you. He will show you how to consistently generate the strength, persistence, and commitment needed to accept and accomplish your life's mission.

Spiritual Stalemate

Spiritual stalemate occurs when we do not remember that we can turn around and look at our lives from a different angle. We forget that we can make different choices. It is as if we become frozen, walking in a fixed direction, our heads unable to turn to the left or right, experiencing only what is directly in front of us.

Beliefs are not objective truth. They are a choice of attitude—the direction we are currently facing. Much like our physical eyes have a limited view of approximately 140 degrees from left to right, so too do our beliefs provide us with a limited range of experience.

Our beliefs are in part formed by our experiences, and our scope of experience is defined by our beliefs. Patterns are established by the recurrent experiences that a particular belief system offers to us. These patterns tend to focus your attention on other experiences that simply reinforce the currently held beliefs. As time passes we can become encrusted and encased within the patterns so that whole areas of life are not available to us. Michael can help you to break through these barriers and patterns so that you can see that life consists of far more than any one particular belief system can encompass.

What benefit does a particular belief system offer you? Does it keep you comfortable or does it facilitate expansion? Ask yourself these questions. They will help you to objectively view different belief systems.

Unlocking Your Belief Systems

On a piece of paper, write down three careers or occupations that you feel you could achieve. Next, write down three careers or occupations that you feel you would not be able to achieve. Take a few moments to write them down.

After you have written down these six occupations or careers, close your eyes. Relax yourself for a few moments. Now go back in time to when you were twelve years old. After a few moments, proceed back to the age ten, then eight, then seven, and finally six years old.

Do you recall playing with your friends when you were six years old? You may have played "pretend." You probably imagined growing up and fulfilling different roles. You saw yourself as a doctor, astronaut, fireman, or perhaps a construction worker operating a large crane. Remember how it felt to imagine those things? Didn't it feel completely possible that you could grow up to fulfill those roles? Why did you believe that you could fulfill those roles?

Now look at your six items. Review the three occupations or careers that you feel you could not achieve. What are the beliefs that are holding you back from fulfilling those roles? Have there been experiences in your life that made you believe that you couldn't move into those roles? Are those beliefs truth? If you really set your energies to the task, couldn't you achieve at least one of the three roles? If not then ask yourself, "why not?"

Belief systems are relative to individuals. For example, a belief system that may provide a specific person a greater set of available experiences may provide another person with a more limited set of available experiences. In most cases, changing a belief system aligns you so that you will have new experiences not afforded to you by the previous belief system.

Belief systems are neither good nor bad. They are self-imposed. With a conscious awareness of how to process your day-to-day experiences from a soul-infused point of view, you can integrate the wisdom of your life and choose to change or modify your beliefs.

For example, you may not believe in the Archangels. This could preclude experiences with them. But you might ask, "How can one believe without experience?" This brings up the attribute of faith. A person may choose to believe something without experiencing it by having faith in it.

There is a danger in accepting a belief system as ultimate truth. For example, imagine you are wearing a pair of glasses that define your field of vision. Perhaps one pair of glasses allows you to see clearly two miles into the distance, but not close up. Another pair of glasses allow you to see close up, but no further than one mile. Yet another may bend the light from the left and right field of vision so that you can see ten miles in either direction. In each case, what you perceive becomes your experience.

Remember that different belief systems open you to different sets of experience. Therefore, choose a belief system for the experience it offers you. From this conscious state you'll be able to prevent self-limiting patterns from being installed in your body/brain system.

Michael helps you to break out of old patterns and belief systems. You can then experience more and more of the creations of the Lord. You have become as the little child again. The very belief that you can have a specific experience will assist you in manifesting that experience in your life.

The Power of Belief

The power of belief is an important element of angelic enlightenment. Work and study along with Michael as he helps you to see the patterns that have been installed within you. The Charting Your Life exercise in chapter 10 was inspired by the Archangel Michael to help you understand what you value, why you value it, and what you believe. As you shine the light of the Sword of Truth on yourself, the process of integrating soul's purpose and pattern has been initiated.

Understanding how your beliefs can define the scope of your experiences is one of the first steps of angelic enlightenment. The Archangel Michael can inspire and guide you through this process. Trust in him and release the tight bands of protective energy that limit your experience. Open yourself to the belief that life can be full of love, wonder, and mystery again. Choose to believe in the Archangels and focus on allowing the attributes of Michael—truth, justice, and honesty—to flower within you.

Realize that you have the symbolic Sword of Truth at your disposal now. You can use it at anytime you choose. Generate the courage to use the sword to cut through your own barriers and illusions. Commit to the process of understanding yourself and uncovering your patterns. Break free from spiritual stalemate. This may be a difficult and challenging process but the Archangel Michael will assist you with his supportive presence and inspire you with his love of truth, honesty, and justice.

It is not power nor desire that are negative,
it is the incorrect application of these attributes that can be negative.

7

Tell the Total Truth:
The Powers, Purpose, and Process of Michael

AS YOU BEGIN working with the Archangel Michael you will gain a greater understanding of the purpose, power, and process that he represents. You become aware of Michael's focus as you journey toward your goal. Like a physical journey to a faraway place, this inner journey will present many new sights to you. These inner sights are, in part, an awareness of the power, purpose, and main process of Michael. As outlined in chapter 1, Michael's main power is seeing, his main process is understanding, and his purpose is the flowering of the Godly attributes of truth, honesty, and justice.

The Power of Seeing

The main power of the energy stream emanating from Michael is symbolized by the Sword of Truth. When the power of this symbolic sword is made evident to the individual, they will find that the scales are removed from their eyes, so to speak. All self-agreed to illusions are laid bare before them.

It is through focusing on the function of seeing that we come to understand our feelings, thoughts, and actions. We do not just hope or pretend that we possess truth, honesty, and justice but rather we strive for clarity in seeing that brings us understanding. This understanding of ourselves manifests in the world in actions that are rooted in the divine attributes of truth, honesty, and justice.

Michael will nudge you to follow the voice of truth within you. This voice is not the voice of your thoughts alone, nor of your heart alone. It is both and more. You assist your self-segments to come into alignment by allowing the divine energy to flow in and out of the centers of your body—receiving then giving. The state of soul-infusion becomes a part of your day-to-day living. From the state of soul-infusion, your seeing power is more refined. You are able to distinguish self-truth from self-deception. When you know that something is not quite right in the way you are viewing a situation or a problem, it is very often because you are reacting to the situation from an imbalance of one or more of the self-segments.

Don't feel bad about this. When we are caught in a storm it is very hard to see with clarity as we try to balance multiple factors while standing upright and continuing to walk. When we work from the state of soul-infusion, it is as if we exist within the eye of the storm, in a place of calm and quiet. It is from here that we can accurately judge our own actions and motivations.

The World is Our Stage

It has been said that "all the world is a stage, and we are its players." From the eye of the storm you can see the stage, identify the players, relate to the roles they play, and appreciate the play itself. The clarity of vision afforded by telling the total truth enables you to make choices that empower and enrich your life.

What part do you play in your world? Are you unsure of your lines? Are you afraid of what's coming next? We can't stop others from acting. That is their freedom, as it is our freedom to act as well. What we can do is find the still, quiet center within us and then present to the world, our loved ones, and ourselves the truth of the spiritual being that we are. This comes from direct experience of ourselves beyond the roles that we play. It comes from an individual experience of enlightenment as we shine the light of seeing upon our worlds.

The power of seeing is like the power of the sun. When we focus the power of seeing upon ourselves, as the sun focuses its light on the earth, we see the reality of our life—devoid of illusions. The shadows are removed. As the light of the sun provides energy for growth and nourishment on earth, so too does focusing on yourself bring you understanding, which provides the energy for the attributes of truth, honesty, and justice to grow on your inner landscape.

The Process of Understanding

Understanding comes as you shine the light of your attention on your experiences. Through repeated viewing of your experiences, you become adept at judging the elements and forces in play around you. The circumstances you find yourself in allow you to learn more about yourself.

As you focus beyond the surface situations to see the energies that have manifested the forms and states in your life, you gain insight into yourself. This insight calms your heart and mind, but the insight that calms can also bring great pain to your heart and mind as you realize your choices may have hurt others as well as yourself.

While it is important to live in the present, we must not forget the lessons of the past so that we do not repeat them again. Heal the pain and live in joy, for life goes on regardless of where we are or what we may be doing. Until we accept that our bodies will die (fourth key to self-knowledge) we cannot fully experience the depth of living that comes from accepting our inherent mortality (seventh key to self-knowledge).

The Purpose of Truth, Honesty, and Justice

The main purpose of the energy stream emanating from this most holy Angel is to assist with the flowering of the Godly attributes of truth, honesty, and justice within each of us. Michael's main purpose is once again symbolized by the scale held in his left hand. All actions require a re-action. Therefore all of our actions will need to be balanced—this is the purpose of the scale. This is known as karma.

Remember that we do not push truth, honesty, and justice upon ourselves or other people. This would be the same as faking a feeling such as false compassion. If we do not feel compassion, then we need to follow the trail of the lack of that emotion back to a past experience to uncover why we do not react in the way that we wish to. The answer truly lies within us and not in another.

If you do not feel like being true to yourself, nor honest—and seem to care more about personal anarchy than about justice—ask yourself why. Usually the answer can be found in your feelings. Once you identify your feelings with the power of seeing, you are ready for the journey to the root emotion. Raphael will assist you to process your feelings and emotions. Michael helps you to see them. Allow yourself to feel. To not allow yourself to feel is dishonoring a part of yourself. Embrace yourself, for healing comes on all levels. We do not chop off parts of our self. We integrate all parts of ourselves. Our experiences will always be our experiences. They can never be erased from our soul's memory.

The Five W's of Telling the Total Truth (Plus: How to Tell the Total Truth)

Telling the total truth does not mean standing on a soapbox and telling everyone around you your life's story and everything that you think, feel, and know. Telling the total truth means to be honest to yourself—tell yourself the total truth! It means to be able to see and accept the choices you make and the patterns that have been established within yourself.

Paradoxically, by telling yourself the total truth, you really tell the whole world the total truth of yourself. The verb *tell* may be misleading here. You don't actually speak words to others, but your reactions to them come from a level of self-honesty that rings true. From that position, they too have the opportunity to respond to you in a like manner. This honesty spirals, building a vortex in the matter worlds for the grace of God to fill.

PETER'S STORY
Telling the Total Truth

During my son's teenage years I reacted to his actions in a very controlling way. This came from my pattern of thinking: "This is the way it is going to be done. Period." His rebellion against conformity was just what I felt as a teenager, only now I was on the other side of the fence.

No matter what I did, or how I responded to him, he seemed to always argue with me. I felt my frustration limit had been reached and I had passed "go" several hundred times!

But then the Archangel Michael began to work with me, as did Raphael. My conversations with my son began to change. By accepting and seeing myself clearly with the help of Michael, I was able to take the next step and show myself clearly—to myself and to my son as well!

One night I recall being paged by my son. I was separated from my ex-wife at the time, which added to the confusion of feelings in general. I found a phone booth and called him to see what he wanted. He needed a ride of some kind. It was 9:00 P.M. on a snowy Sunday evening. He knew from our previous agreement that if he needed a ride he would give me at least one day's notice.

I was tired and I didn't feel like driving across town to transport him to a friend's house, but was worried that he would be angry with me if I told him that. I began explaining that I didn't want to drive him and he reacted from the old patterns of arguing that we used to fall into. Instead of arguing back and telling him "no" over and over again, I told him in the most honest way how I felt: "I feel bad when I have to tell you no, but I am just very tired tonight and I need to stay home." To my surprise he grew quiet and responded, "oh, ok." End of argument or any hard feelings.

That simple conversation with my son was both an enlightening experience and a turning point in my understanding of the power of seeing and the benefits of telling the total truth.

What is the Total Truth?

Telling the total truth is an important step in the alignment of the self-segments. The total truth is reflected in the totality of all your experiences—processed, unprocessed, and integrated. It is the reality of God as you have experienced it. In this light, all life's experiences are sacred—they are from God's universe born of the Creator's loving essence. So in truth, you are of that loving essence and are a being of love living in the total truth of the Creator. Michael asks us to light the lamp of divinity within us so that we can have the power to see ourselves once again—so that we may share ourselves with the world once again—in peace and harmony.

When Should You Tell the Total Truth?

Tell yourself the total truth every morning, noon, and night. Tell yourself the total truth at all times and in all ways while watching for the egocentric self's tendencies to misinterpret experiences toward its own end. Learn to understand the egocentric self's tendencies. They are not wrong or evil! They point to a truth that lies beneath their survival-based reactions. Therefore, when you become aware that a part of you is hiding the truth of yourself and your reactions, do not condemn or shun that part! Rather, shine the light of soul's love on it to bring it from a place of fear to a place of acceptance. You will become a law unto yourself and a being of light, peace, balance, and feeling.

Tell the total truth each moment and you will live a life filled with contentment. Your choices will be honest, any heartache will be pure, and your tears will be as the hand of God upon your shoulder. Your smiles will be as the sun rising to light the darkness.

Where is the Total Truth?

This is best understood by another question: "Where are you?" The total truth is the current state of integrated wisdom that resides in the wisdom pool of the higher self combined with the unprocessed or partially processed experiences that reside in our soul's memory. The total truth is found in our willingness to admit and begin the process of integration and wisdom gathering. This willingness is a trust. This means that your soul self, through the messages and impulses of all the selves, will call upon you to manifest the courage to live.

Why Should You Tell the Total Truth?

Do you want love, peace, understanding, and happiness in your life and that of your loved ones? Do you want to live every day with the wonder of life that you felt as a small child? These reasons and more are why you should always tell the total truth to yourself and others.

A lie may be easier to tell in a specific moment. Yet as you close yourself to a bit of the truth by lying to yourself, you only momentarily cover that which must be uncovered someday anyway. You postpone your growth.

Remember, as your body breathes in and then out, and as your body rests and then plays, so too do you process and then integrate wisdom. Experience, then ponder. Allow the wisdom of the higher self and the guidance of the soul self to bring answers to your conscious self so that you may incorporate them into your daily living.

How to Tell the Total Truth

Here are a few ways to tell the total truth:

1. **Listen to your conscience.** Listen to that small, still voice within yourself. It is there for a reason. It is the voice of your soul self sending its impulses to you to guide you in fulfilling soul's pattern and purpose.

2. **Practice Charting Your Life.** This exercise was inspired by the Archangel Michael. It can help you identify areas that need further understanding and processing for wisdom gathering.

3. **Say the prayers and invoke the presence of Michael.** This helps you to focus on seeing with clarity and gives you the inspiration to continue. Remember to be kind to yourself during this process.

4. **Use the meditations in this book.** These exercises, particularly those in chapter 9, will help you place your attention on the process of understanding yourself through the power of seeing.

5. **Just try it ... you'll like it!** After you tell yourself the total truth, you can relax. All the things that you worried about happening which caused you to suppress yourself usually don't occur anyway, or if they do they are not as tragic or dramatic as you thought they would be—plus life may just surprise you as well!

Start Today!

Start telling the total truth today—tomorrow may be too late. None of us know when we will leave this stage or when our loved ones will leave this stage of life. Speak to them now from the truth that you are. Share the truth of yourself that is within your heart. Allow them to share themselves (all that they can) and accept and learn from what they share with you. Thank them for their love and love them in return.

Telling the total truth is a life-long process that starts the moment you become aware that you are alive. Look to Michael. Hold the Sword of Truth with courage and determination. Hold it with a healthy self-love that comes from the grace of God and from your own desire to learn and grow.

By following the trail of our desires
we begin our journey of self-discovery.

8

A Message from Michael

Understanding and Integrating Soul's Pattern

I come in truth and truth I show to you. It is the truth that you have ignored for so long. It is the truth that you knew was always within you, deep inside your being. It is the truth that you've forgotten as you've lost contact with your innocence.

I ask those who seek my assistance to generate the courage to face themselves without their masks of protection. You need courage to feel the pain of the experiences that you have neglected to process. You also need a strong desire to know yourself.

The ancients have said, "Man know thyself." But how can you know yourself until you understand why you choose to do what you do? Until you understand the motivating factors of your life, you will be swayed from experience to experience, never knowing how the trail of your life was forged.

I bring before you the scales of justice so that all men may know the truth of the Creator. I bring forth before you the scales of justice so that you will understand that every action requires a reaction in the worlds of energy, matter, space, and time. This reaction is not punitive. This reaction is part of the cyclical nature of the earth world.

If called upon, I shall not falter. I shall point to your side where resides the Sword of Truth awaiting your acceptance. With the symbolic Sword of Truth you are now empowered to see your true motivations and come to understand yourself.

No longer will you choose to look at your experiences and make decisions based only on self-interest. No longer will you rationalize the obvious to support belief systems that you have placed your interest in.

Experience is why the soul chose to spin the embodiments that you are now conscious of. This experience is for the benefit of the integrated self. It is a gift from God. Cherish it and honor it with the respect that it is due. Each and every form has its purpose, and each and every form has its function. All of these are given life by the pure energy of the Creator.

How can you come to understand soul's pattern? The process that the four Archangels will lead you through is a process of self-discovery, healing, commitment, and love.

Men and women of the earth, look to the truth of the love in your hearts. I have no power to unmask you. Nor do I push or pull or prod or coddle. To see yourself in the true light is at once to be startled and shocked, while at the same time to be relieved. As you accept the divine energy as manifested through the attributes of truth, honesty, and justice—your old self (the self that was constructed by your old patterns) begins to break away. Underneath is the tender part of who you are; fresh, alive, and willing to live life to its fullest. I ask you to open up to the fullness of life, to the tenderness of your true self in order to manifest greater clarity, truth, and love into your world.

The Archangels' plan of healing is a simple plan. There is nothing you need to purchase. There is no one you need to seek and there are no qualifications that restrict you from benefiting from this plan. There are requirements, but these requirements are only guidelines. In order for you to expand, you must move; and in order for you to move, you must motivate yourself.

Understanding soul's purpose lies in understanding soul's pattern. Everything is as it should be at this moment of time including the fact that you are now deciding to become a conscious integrated being on all levels: from the soul self through the higher self, through the conscious, the emotional, and the basic selves.

To each in its own time, and to each time a purpose. With this purpose comes the information to assist you in removing the scales from your eyes so that you may begin to consciously choose your course of action; to heal the wounds of the past that keep your heart from being open to life and its wonders; to commit with persistence and with unending strength to accomplishing your life's purpose on multiple levels; and in, before, during, and after all things and events of this world—to appreciate, to love, and to be.

To be true, one must admit to the feelings that one has. Raphael will help you to accept your emotions and to learn from your desires. By admitting to the emotions that you are feeling, you can remove the barriers from around you. Deeper and deeper levels of honesty require you to show more and more of yourself to yourself and to the world. A deeper understanding of justice will lead you to accept the cycles of experience you have chosen. And deeper levels of strength and commitment will help you to carry through with soul's purpose and your life's mission.

I come to you to offer you the chalice of purity, and as you drink of it, you drink of your own truth, accepting and nourishing from the inner truth that is you. Accept my help, for I give it freely. Turn your head toward the Heavens, for God cares for you. Fear not, for the Angels and the Archangels are as near as your heartbeat. Remember this as you strive to connect to the wisdom pool of your higher self and to the loving guidance of the soul self.

I come not to show you the truth of others' lives. I come to show you the way to see the truth of your own life. How else can you change until you look at the reality of how your life has been constructed? How else can you move and grow until you break the barriers that bind your energy centers? The task of seeing the truth and looking into the mirror of truth is not for the timid. The attribute of strength is needed. As I guide you, you can also ask the other Archangels to inspire you in manifesting their divine attributes.

Raphael assists you with healing, acceptance, and wholeness. If you look into the mirror of truth and you are not able to heal, you will be distressed by the truth that you see. If you look into the mirror of truth and you are not able to accept what you see, you will cease your search for the inner truth. If you look into the mirror of truth without understanding the wholeness of life, you will pity yourself.

Gabriel assists you with strength, persistence, and commitment. If you begin to look at the truth of yourself but have no commitment you will stop. If you begin to look at the truth of yourself and have no strength you will falter, and if you begin to look at the truth of yourself and have no persistence your efforts will last only a short time and you may not reach that which you desire.

Uriel assists you with love, beauty, and appreciation. If you look into the mirror of truth without love you will feel contempt for yourself. If you look into the mirror of truth without seeing the beauty of the negative and positive, you will fail to understand the forces that push and pull you to your destiny. If you look into the mirror of truth and fail to appreciate your life you will have gained nothing.

It is with all the attributes of our Creator (as manifested through the purpose and powers of the four Archangels) that you search, see, accept, and integrate all truth. I will assist you to see the truth of thyself and in it you will see the truth of your creations. This will give you great joy throughout this transformational process of integration.

This message I have brought to you through the universal Christ energy of the Creator.

Deeper and deeper levels of honesty require you to show more and more of yourself to yourself and to the world.

9

Prayers and Meditations to Contact the Archangel Michael

A Prayer on Honesty

Dear Michael,

Help me to achieve the honesty required to live a life of truth and justice. Stay with me as I strive to break free of my self-constructed patterns. Send me your energy as I choose to consciously change my life to be more honest in word, expression, and deed.

This I ask of you through the universal Christ energy, Amen.

MEDITATION

On Michael's Presence

Take a seat in an easy chair or lie on a bed. Loosen any tight fitting clothes. Use the method you are best suited to for relaxation (such as deep breathing). This will help you focus inwardly. Make sure that you will not be disturbed for 15 to 30 minutes. After your mind has quieted and your body is relaxed, continue with the rest of the meditation.

You find yourself standing in a temple. It is light and spacious. The floors are shiny marble and there are large columns spread throughout its interior. You feel safe here and know that it is a good place.

There is no one else around, so you decide to explore the temple for yourself. You open a large stone door and enter a room. You see several tables. There are many ornate boxes sitting on the tables. You go over to one of the tables and open a beautiful hand-carved box. Inside you see gems of all kinds. They sparkle. Another box is filled with gold and silver coins.

You notice a wooden door at the end of the room and walk over to it. You open the door and walk through it into another room. This room is as nice as the first. It is empty except for the bookshelves that are on each of its four walls. The bookshelves reach from floor to ceiling. Every row of each bookshelf is crowded with books. As you look closer you see that the books are all written by well-known philosophers, thinkers, and mystics. Most of the books are covered with dust.

You see another door and walk over to it. It is made of glass. It swings easily as you open it. You enter a room that is empty except for an altar directly in front of you. As you walk toward the altar you notice a large mirror on the wall behind the altar. You reach the altar and look into the mirror. You see yourself. Look at yourself for a while in this room.

You hear a voice from behind you. You turn to see Michael, carrying a chalice in his right hand and a sword in his left. He walks toward you and offers you the chalice. You take it slowly and look into it. You see water. You begin to drink, amazed at the taste of the water. It is unlike any water you have tasted before. You look into Michael's eyes. Take a moment to relax in Michael's presence. Ask him questions if you wish.

After a time, you and Michael leave the room together. As you return to the room with the wooden door, you notice that the room is now completely empty. There are no longer any bookshelves on the walls! Next, you move into the room with the stone door and notice that the boxes are no longer on the tables as they were. In fact, there are no tables in the room at all. You now leave the stone room and enter into the main sanctuary of the temple. You are alone again.

After a while thank Michael, and slowly open your eyes. Relax and allow the presence of Michael to be with you as you ponder the meaning of your experience.

A Prayer on Truth

Dear Michael,

I pray to you to help me to lift the scales from my eyes and my mind. I know that I have hidden the truth of myself from myself for so long. I am now ready to come forward without fear. I commit to reveal the full truth of who I am in a loving and caring way. This I ask of you through the universal Christ energy, Amen.

MEDITATION

On Truth

Take a seat in an easy chair or lie on a bed. Loosen any tight fitting clothes. Use the method you are best suited to for relaxation (such as deep breathing). This will help you focus inwardly. Make sure that you will not be disturbed for 15 to 30 minutes. After your mind has quieted and your body is relaxed, continue with the rest of the meditation.

Imagine that you are standing in front of a large mirror. The mirror spans the whole length of a wall—almost sixteen feet. In the center of the mirror you see yourself as you are today in present life. You are dressed in your normal fashion and are in a relaxed state.

Now think of yourself as a baby, a newborn. Take a moment and "feel" being newborn . . . next take the image of yourself as a newborn and "place" it in the mirror to the far left of center. Now as you look into the mirror you see two images: one of yourself as a newborn infant and one of yourself in the present time.

Next think of yourself as a toddler walking around your home. Once again take a moment to feel yourself as a toddler. Now take the image of yourself as a toddler and place it next to the image of the newborn infant in the mirror. From left to right, you should now see the newborn image of yourself, the toddler image of yourself, and finally the image of yourself in present time.

Now, in succession, move five years ahead. With each succession think of yourself at that particular age. Make sure to take a moment and "feel" yourself at that age. Also make sure to take an image of yourself at that age and "place" it in the mirror next to the previous image. Keep doing this step (moving forward five years at a time and placing an image in the mirror) until you reach your current age.

Take a moment to scan all the images in the mirror.

Now move back from the mirror. To your surprise, as you move back, your present day image stays in the same place within the mirror. You are now independent from the images in the mirror. You are in the soul self's viewpoint. You are a unit of awareness.

From this vantage point, review each of the images in the mirror again. With each image and progression of the images—from youth to your present age—try to see how your personality for this life was formed. Each self image contains the seeds that created it. It has manifested from your memory banks and is now in the mirror for your review.

Allow yourself, from this detached viewpoint, to come to view with honesty the choices you have made and the experiences that occurred at each time juncture. Try to uncover the values that you held, and how they were formed at each juncture. How did you associate your experience to cause and effect and process it to form beliefs? Where did those beliefs come from? Have your experiences been fully processed? Can you see them differently now? Can further processing help you grow?

Do this for a while, about 10 to 15 minutes. Don't stay too long. You can always come back and explore more anytime you wish—for all this is inside you always. The goal of this meditation is to uncover how your personality and general viewpoint of life has been formed so that you may view the truth of yourself and begin to change elements of your values and beliefs. Understanding your values and beliefs helps you to make conscious choices in the present. This is one meaning of free will—to choose while knowing how your beliefs affect your life's experiences.

A Prayer on Justice

Dear Michael,

I pray to you to assist me as I foster a true and loving compassion within my being by accepting my humanity. I promise to be kind and show mercy when it is my place to do so. I also promise to be just in my dealings with all men on earth and in Heaven. Continue to be with me, Michael, and teach me more about justice each and every day.

This I ask of you through the universal Christ energy, Amen.

You are alive in a sea of God's energy.

10

Charting Your Life:
An Exercise with Michael

DUE TO THE speed at which most people live their lives in the modern world, life often seems like a blur. The sun rises and sets, and every moment in between is filled with some duty or responsibility. It is no wonder that for many, life seems to be passing them by. The Charting Your Life exercise helps you to slow down so that you can focus on reviewing this experience called life.

This exercise, inspired by the Archangel Michael, involves both objective and subjective evaluation. Using these two methods of evaluation, the Charting Your Life exercise provides a balanced and effective method to view your life in a new way.

The exercise asks you to choose a subject of interest, a judgment scale to evaluate it by, and the time frame to be covered. We have found that this exercise is most easily accomplished by the use of a traditional x/y coordinate graph. Refer to the *Charting Your Life Subject Scale Sheet* for a moment (page 76). The horizontal coordinates at the bottom of the graph delineate the time frame (time-segments), and the vertical coordinates to the left of the graph delineate the judgment scale.

For example, you can use the exercise to evaluate your spiritual life over a period of time. In this case, the subject of the chart would be "spiritual fulfillment." The highest rating on the scale, a ten, would represent "most fulfilled spiritually" and the lowest rating on the scale, a one, would represent "least fulfilled spiritually." The twelve available time-segments at the bottom of the graph could be in years. In this example, you would write in *1976* under the first time-segment, *1978* under the second time segment, and so on in two-year increments through the twelfth time segment. After choosing your subject, setting up your scale, and deciding on the time frame, you are ready to continue the exercise.

Starting with the earliest time segment (in this case, 1976) choose a number from one to ten that best represents how you would rate the time-segment according to your scale (spiritual fulfillment). Place a dot on the graph where the time-segment and scale rating intersect. Perform this step with all the time-segments on your chart. After you are done, draw a line between each dot on the chart. You can then easily see the flow of this particular subject over time.

The next step is to take an *Events and Observation* sheet and fill one out for the subject that you have just graphed (spiritual fulfillment in our example). You will notice that this sheet has two sides—A and B. The sections on the sheet start at event 1 notes and end at event 12 notes. Side A provides space for you to write about the first six time-segments (event 1 notes through event 6 notes), and side B provides space for the last six (event 7 notes through event 12 notes).

Starting with event 1 notes, think of any major events that occurred in your life during that time segment. Write down anything of significance that comes to you. Now review how you rated that time-segment on your judgment scale. Consider your rating and events during that time-segment and record your observations. This shows you the mixture of the subjective and objective elements of this exercise. The subjective element is your feeling about the subject for that time-segment in the form of a numeric rating. The objective element is your detailing of events in that time-segment and your observations of the correlation between rating and events.

After filling out the event 1 notes section, proceed to fill out all the remaining event notes sections in the manner described. You may have fewer time-segments to chart. If you do, then just fill out the event notes that apply to your time-frame. If you wish to have more time-segments than are available on the graph form you can extend the graph on another sheet of paper—improvise if needed.

The exercise also allows you to vary the time-segments to fit the subject. The time-segments do not have to be bi-yearly as in our example. They could be yearly, monthly, or even daily. In some cases, they may be hourly! Here is an example in where it makes sense to use hourly time-segments: Let's say there was a culmination of events that resulted in a serious argument with your spouse or partner. How can you figure out what caused the argument? Can you piece together the events of the day? Many times the events of the day pass so quickly that we cannot remember them well. It is also possible that strong emotions make it difficult to objectively view what has occurred. This is where the graph and events sheets will help.

Take out a chart. Place today's date and time on the sheet. Write in the subject as: *Argument with Spouse.* Write in scale ten as "most argumentative." Write in scale one as "least argumentative." Now that you've set your subject and your judgment scale you need to set your time frame (time-segments).

In this example, you recall that the argument hits its strongest point at about 6:00 P.M. Start time segment one at 10:00 A.M., and go forward in hourly increments, writing the time in the appropriate space on the horizontal graph line. Now you should rate each of the hourly periods against your judgment scale by placing a dot on the graph where applicable.

Take an *Events and Observations* sheet and write down what was happening in each of the time segments. Write down events, how you were feeling, thoughts that came to your mind, and so forth. Next, review what you have written and look for cause and effect within the events.

This exercise is designed to help you uncover your own motivations and the part you played in relation to the subject of the graph. We have given you a couple of ways to use the forms. It is important that you take time to review all that you have written as you fill out the events and observations. Look for links between your events and your feelings.

A way to increase the benefits of this exercise is to do multiple subjects for the same time period. For example, you may wish to chart your spiritual fulfillment over a ten year period, as well as your marriage over the same period of years if applicable. You can even add more subject layers—such as a chart on your physical health—for that same time frame. After filling out all three graphs and events sheets, set them side by side and review them. Start to look for patterns. Take out some blank sheets of paper and write down any patterns you begin to see.

Charting Your Life
Subject Scale Sheet

Date: __2-4-98__   Time: __6:30p.m.__

Subject: __Spiritual Fulfillment__

Scale 10: __Most fulfilled spiritually__

Scale 1: __Least fulfilled spiritually__

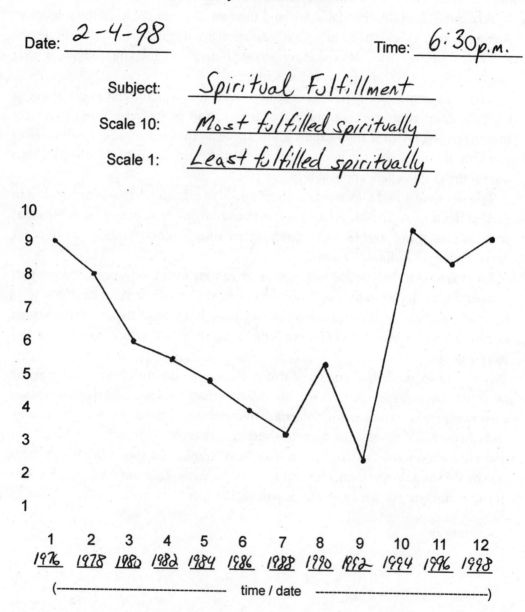

Note: The numbers on the left of the graph relate to the scale as filled in at top. The numbers at the bottom of the graph are time/date slices. The lines under each time/date slice are for you to enter the time and/or date that the number represents (i.e. 1 = Jan 98, 2 = Feb 98, etc.).

Charting Your Life

Events and Observations: Side A

Date: __2-4-98__   Subject: __Spiritual Fulfillment__

Event 1 notes—Was living at home w/father. Going to college part-time. Work only summer jobs. Deeply involved in spiritual path. Trying new spiritual techniques for OBE given by path. Future looked bright. Strong belief I had found "true" path to God. No debts—few responsibilities. Believed leader of path was the highest consciousness on Earth. Received initiation on path.

Event 2 notes—Married 1st time. Quit college. First child born. Became involved in path's local organization. Received another initiation. Expected more conscious spiritual experiences as promised by path's writings + leader. Started working full-time. Saw evidence that current leader of path took sections of writings from deceased founder's book for his writings without credit.

Event 3 notes. Hard financial times. Moved whole family back in w/father for 3 months, then w/grandparents for 3 months. New leader took over path in friendly transition. Looked forward to new growth and the promised conscious spiritual experiences.

Event 4 notes. Started small home-based business. Began drinking often. Got extended on credit bills. Separated from wife for short time. Stopped drinking in March '83. Hard financial times in Summer '83. Lucrative short term position late '83. Received another initiation on the path.

Event 5 notes Previous leader of path was ex-communicated by current leader for alleged misappropriation of path funds. Founder of path was shown to have taken large amounts of writings intact from path he previously studied under + sold those writings as his own. Lame excuses made by current leader of path for this behavior. Spouse wouldn't view this issue. I felt I had to drop this issue to maintain family stability. 2nd child born w/health problems.

Event 6 notes—Struggled through various jobs, not much money. Moved across country to be near special clinic for 2nd child's therapy. Financial boost w/new job in 1987. Long hours—much driving. Enjoyed work. Found people from path in new area to be different. Became aware of infighting, backbiting, + elitism among path's local leaders.

Charting Your Life

Events and Observations: Side B

Date: 2-4-98   Subject: Spiritual Fulfillment

Event 7 notes—Received another initiation to become priest/clergy of path. Kept working at good paying job. Long hours. Decided to move to path's main headquarter's city in 1989. I was resistant to move, spouse was insistent. Moved. Took lower paying job. Bought 1st home. Struggled to fit in at new job. Local path people were nice. Path building first church structure. Special time.

Event 8 notes
Church opened. Was not invited to opening. Could not get better work position. Finally moved to better position in late '91. Church would not let me teach a class at church structure. Felt rejected. Step-child w/teenage issues. 2nd child underwent hip surgery—much pain.

Event 9 notes—Marriage strain getting worse. 1st child having trouble w/authority in school. Path's leader's talks were boring and redundant. No new information seemed to come from path's teachings. 2nd child underwent hip surgeries '92 & '83. Again much pain. Infighting in Church now more apparent. Employee of the year 1993 at work.

Event 10 notes—Separated from spouse 4/94. Major project at work failed. New job Oct-94, much potential. Hard summer alone from family. Allowed myself to read other books rather than only path's books and path's reading list. Lost 40 pounds. Opened my horizons to other views. Began to feel joy again. Met Linda 9/94. Creative flow strong. Many songs written. High Consciousness. Felt the presence of ArchAngel Michael.

Event 11 notes—Divorce finalized. Many difficult details to handle. Saw leader of path trying to control followers. Began to view/see him as a human and not as the highest consciousness on earth. Angry at the wasted years in path. Struggled w/belief systems and the purpose of life. Felt Raphael's presence. Married Linda in 1997. Bought home. Formally started The Circle of Angelic Enlightenment. Created website: WWW.ANGELIC-CIRCLE.COM. Began writing books.

Event 12 notes
Spiritual purpose clear again. Moving forward w/physical and spiritual goals. Gabriel's presence felt late '97. Uriel's influence starting in '98. Realized within me is the key to my own enlightenment and healing.

This exercise can help you to understand yourself and your motivations. It helps you to recognize what you value and believe. By seeing what you value and believe, you come to understand the connections between those things and your daily experiences. As you begin to see connections between what you value and what you experience, as well as connections between what you experience and what you believe, you start to come to a more conscious awareness of how these factors interplay in your life. No longer will your thoughts be muddled about what an event or situation means. No longer will you be confused about how and why you reacted to those events and situations as they occurred.

You may be surprised by what you begin to uncover. During the exercise you must be honest both subjectively and objectively. Subjectively place yourself in the time period in order to relate to the events and feelings of that time. Then take yourself into the present time to make your observations. It is usually accepted as true that the more experiences we have, the greater is our awareness. The greater our awareness, the greater is our ability to analyze our past, learn from it, process it, and integrate it as wisdom stored in our higher self.

Before you start this exercise it is good to relax for a short time. Due to the hectic pace of modern living we are constantly moving and doing. When you feel overburdened with doing, try the following short technique. This technique will help you slow the pace of your thoughts so that you can focus.

Have you ever tried to just breathe in or to just breathe out? If you are able, try right now to breathe out three breaths for every breath you take in. Do not attempt this if it causes you undue strain. If you can't physically do this, then imagine what it would feel like to do so. Breathing like this is what it feels like to constantly be doing, doing, doing, never taking back in the breath of life to rejuvenate ourselves.

Now, imagine that you are breathing in one breath for every exhaled breath. Do this for three or four cycles. Next imagine that you are breathing not air into your lungs, but rather life into your body, mind, and spirit. Breathe in the colors and sights around you. Take in the world, through your perceptions. Give room in your being and energy centers to accept in the world; then focus back outward and give back out the energy. If you are always focused outward, an imbalance occurs. Confusion can result from this imbalance. By using this short relaxation technique, you can balance the energy flowing in and out of your body. Do this relaxation technique before trying the Charting Your Life exercise or at anytime during your day when you start to feel confused and cluttered in your thinking.

Remember the love and presence of the Archangel Michael as you work with the Charting Your Life exercise. With it you can learn more about yourself, your life, and the motivations and energies that push and pull you into action. You can also uncover experiences from the past that may not be fully processed. Very often there are painful memories hidden in past experiences that we have not yet processed. This exercise can uncover them for you. Use the L.E.A.R.N. technique of Raphael, presented in the next section, to process these memories. Remember that experience is the fuel that propels our growth.

Much love is given to us and much love is expected. May you unfold in peace, love, and care. And may this exercise inspired by the Archangel Michael assist you in the process of living.

The proof is in the processing.

Section 3

The Archangel Raphael

I am Raphael, one of the seven holy angels,
which present the prayers of the saints,
and which go in and out
before the glory of the Holy One.

—The Book of Tobit 12:15

11

Raphael: The Archangel of Healing and Acceptance

THE NEXT ARCHANGEL to make his presence known to you is Saint Raphael. He is most recognized as the Angel who helped young Tobias on his journey. He is especially fond of travelers and is usually pictured in sandaled feet with a walking staff in his left hand. Raphael assists you with healing the wounds that you are uncovering with the power of seeing. These wounds often remain covered and unprocessed for months and sometimes years. With Raphael's help, you will learn ways to process the emotions so that you can feel them in their completeness. Without feeling the emotions, you cannot fully express them, and without expressing them you cannot heal the pain and integrate the knowledge within them. They remain as scars upon your heart.

Allowing Yourself to Fully Feel

Think back to when you were very young. Go back through the years. Can you recall a time when you were hurt emotionally? This could have been an experience with a friend or a reaction to your parents about something you did or did not do. What did you feel? Did you cover yourself with a bandage? Did you respond honestly? How was your response received and how were you responded to in return?

It is in the response to our experiences that we are faced with the challenge of expressing and not repressing. Expressing means to accurately respond to the experience via self-truth. When faced with a painful experience we are confronted with the instinctive urge to pull our heart back into a shell, much as a turtle pulls its arms and legs into its shell for protection.

What happens to you when you put your heart in a shell? You stop feeling and you stop expressing. Without expressing, healing cannot occur—nor can we achieve the wholeness that comes from that healing. We begin to believe that life hurts; that to share ourselves with others is painful. As Christ said, "Turn the other cheek." By turning the other cheek you consciously forego the instinctual reaction to cover and retaliate. The action of turning the other check is as much for yourself as it is for those who strike you.

Uncovering Your Heart Again

The fear of loss combined with misinterpretation of our experiences caused by the self-interest of the egocentric self (or the insecurities of the shadow self) has driven us to close off our heart center. This combination has made strange and mysterious pathways to our heart, which makes it more difficult for other people to connect with us and for us to connect with them.

We uncover our heart to experience the fullness of life again by removing the bandages and coverings we have placed around it. These bandages were temporary fixes. They were intended to help us get through another day here on earth. They were not meant to become chains to hold us in fear. The first step to removing the bandages from around our heart is to shine the light of truth on them. Very often the shock of seeing the truth of our lives will scare us back into comfortable patterns of hiding from our experiences. We must resist that urge for without the power to feel the pain, we cannot heal and dissolve the scar.

The next step is to completely, accurately, and constructively express your feelings. This allows the golden essence of love to soothe and heal the scars. By allowing yourself to fully feel the joy and the pain of your experiences, you honor your life, the lives of those around you, and the Creator.

Raphael's presence and energy gives you support as you continue the healing process. Raphael will be with you to help you to break free. The Angels and

Archangels are here to help. After we have experienced the positive healing effect that self-acceptance brings us, our desire to continue toward uncovering more and more of our heart increases.

Expressing is not Suppressing

Expressing our feelings means expressing them all—not suppressing them. It's not enough to just express our feelings. We must express them in a way that is constructive and continues the healing process.

Expressing in a way that is hurtful and destructive to ourselves and others should be avoided. If you have these urges don't feel bad, it just means that you haven't fully processed the emotion. The L.E.A.R.N. technique can help you to process an emotion to the root level. This technique also teaches us how to express our emotions in ways that promote understanding of ourselves and others. This brings wholeness and eventual acceptance of life in all its aspects. For example, if someone says something that hurts you, it is natural to feel sadness. For many, the sadness is quickly replaced by anger. While some will not respond directly, others will immediately respond in retaliatory anger. By choosing a mode that is designed to hurt, they believe that the other person will understand their feelings—or at least that the other person will be suffering as they themselves are.

Still others will strive to drill deeper past the emotion of anger to the underlying emotions. Emotions have root emotions. Anger has layers beneath it that lead to its root emotion. When we become aware of the root emotion behind the apparent (surface) emotion, we tend to communicate better. We choose to phrase our words in a non-threatening way that better describes what we are experiencing and feeling.

For example, let's say that someone at work always cuts you off in mid-sentence during conversations. What can you do? You could choose to ignore it, or you could choose to cut them off in response. You may attack them verbally—to their face or behind their back. However, if you wish to communicate in constructive ways, you may choose to express yourself clearly such as:

"When you cut me off in mid-sentence I feel as though you don't care what I think. I am hurt that you don't appear to value my opinion."

Compare the following statement with the previous one. How do you think someone would respond to each of the statements?

"It really pisses me off that you cut me off all the time. I think that you're a jerk and I'm tired of your stupid opinions!"

The L.E.A.R.N. technique of Raphael provides a step-by-step approach for processing your feelings and emotions as they relate to your experiences. Remember that the main purpose of feeling and expressing is to grow the attributes of wholeness, acceptance, and healing. The energy of these attributes helps to keep us open to the Holy Spirit, the soul self, and the wisdom of our higher self. This in turn builds a warm protective environment in which to live.

To "love thy neighbor" is to give him respect and to love yourself is to honor and respect your own experience. The greatest honor we can give life is to choose to process to the maximum fullness each experience we have while extracting the pearls of wisdom from within these experiences. This extracted wisdom is stored in the higher self. It is shared through your open heart in an honest and natural way—when you feel it! No longer do you need to strive to be spiritual or holy. You get to feel those feelings when you really do feel them. The purifying process of proper expression brings these divine attributes to you in a natural and balanced way.

The Repression Pressure Cooker

The years of repression, fueled by the egocentric self's fear of rejection and loss, create a ticking time bomb within us. This time bomb is sort of a deep-frying pressure cooker—the "repression pressure cooker." As the emotions are ignored, their energy is stuffed into the pressure cooker, creating a progressively more volatile situation.

The recurrent repression of emotion also leads to communication difficulties—simply because we have decided that we can't be honest with those around us. When we are not honest with others, we cannot expect them to respond to us from a position of accuracy—thus compounding the problem. Eventually the load and pressure becomes too strong and the cooker explodes or begins to let off hot compressed steam.

With the help of Archangel Michael we learn to uncover the truth of our repression in self-honesty. While it is a difficult task, we nevertheless must admit that we alone have hidden the truth about ourselves from ourselves for so long. We begin to view the falsehoods that we had accepted as truth. We also begin to see how we have contorted our hearts by allowing our fears to control us. As we begin to process repressed experiences, pressure is released from the cooker. Seeing the truth of the "repression pressure cooker" and admitting that it exists can hurt us even more. We realize in stark somberness how we have spent precious years spinning in patterns of unhappiness and desensitization. In many ways we may have been living life like zombies—unable to feel into the deepness of our hearts where the connection with our humanity and our divinity lies.

The Layers of Emotions

By understanding ourselves and the emotions (see chapter 28) we can deal constructively and positively with any feeling, including anger, envy, jealousy, and the rest of the so-called negative emotions. The new hurt of realizing that we have spent years in repression—years that we cannot recapture—can be mixed with anger. Remember that there are no right or wrong emotions. We feel what we feel. We get to feel all of our emotions and learn from them—including our anger and other negative or uncomfortable emotions. The following is a short example of the layers of emotions that we can experience:

- Someone criticizes you. You react in anger.

- Underneath the anger is the next deeper layer of emotion, which is hurt. You have been hurt because you feel their criticism is partially correct.

- Continuing deeper, you feel sadness. You have failed to live up to that person's expectation (or your own expectation).

- Finally, you go to the deepest layer or root emotion, which is fear. You fear the loss of the other person's love, as well as the fear beneath that—that you are unworthy of love.

Additional information on how to find the root emotion is covered in the L.E.A.R.N. technique (described later in this section). It is part and parcel of the process of effectively expressing the feelings that you have.

Emotional Limbo

Do you ever wonder why you do not feel a particular emotion in a specific situation? For example, in a situation where you believe the emotion of compassion would be logical, you end up feeling superiority instead. Or you may feel contempt rather than love for humanity. Why do you feel jealousy rather than contentment? It is of no avail for us to attempt to dictate our feelings to ourselves. It simply doesn't work. Regardless of the many rules, laws, proclamations, and doctrines made by spiritual paths downgrading certain negative emotions, we cannot succeed in feeling the corresponding positive emotions by sheer willpower. Following the laws and rules of spiritual paths cannot in and of itself cause us to feel the glorious emotions of spiritual fulfillment and human contentment.

When we place our willpower on viewing our self-truth, then we provide ourselves with the opportunity to feel the flip side of the negative emotions. Thus, emotion is seen as a vibration. As you would feel the vibrations of someone tapping on the far side of a wall and follow the vibrations of their tapping to align yourself with them, you can follow the tapping of your emotions. This will help you feel, see, and know the next step that you need to take. When we have a desire to learn and grow by fully processing our life's experiences to the deepest levels, we act from a state of acceptance. In a most natural way we have miraculously returned to the child-like state of wonder. We begin to feel glorious feelings as the energy of life pulses through our heart center. This is made manifest in our actions, words, and deeds so gracefully that we are in awe of the efficiency and care of the Holy Spirit.

Identifying Repression

We all know that we will die someday. Our bodies will cease to function in the manner that they have been since the day we were born onto this earth. The following exercise is intended to help you focus on how to identify repression by using the topic of mortality (seventh key to self-knowledge).

Identifying Repression

Relax and make sure that it is quiet and you can concentrate. As you read each sentence, be sure to pause and reread the sentence over at least once:

- Your body will someday be dead.

- It will disintegrate into dust.

- This dust will blow across the earth to be reshaped into other forms.

Next, identify your feelings by writing down three thoughts on each of the above sentences. Write down what you feel. If you can't feel, then you either aren't focusing or you are refusing to release your repression. In writing down your feelings, you have begun to express yourself.

Finally, reread each of the three initial sentences and your three thoughts. Sit, think, and ponder about what you have written. Can you accept these thoughts? Were you able to feel your feelings? How does it feel to feel those feelings?

Since there seems to be no objective proof of life after death, assume (for the sake of this exercise) that there may actually be nothing after death. As you perform this exercise, be watchful of your tendency to repress your feelings in regard to this possibility. Death is an experience of life. To accept our death is to accept our life. To deny one experience is to take away from the wholeness of all. We gain a deep appreciation of our humanity when we paradoxically accept our mortality and reveal our heart to the world around us.

Take a few minutes to try the above exercise with three issues from the present. The issues that you should pick to review are issues that you know are in your "repression pressure cooker." These issues are probably issues that you are afraid of. Write the three issues down and follow the steps outlined on page 89. These are issues for you to work on and to process.

Explore your feelings. They can lead you to answers and new ways of viewing life. This will in turn open up your energy centers with the precious awareness of the nowness of the eternal moment in which we all live, move, and have our being.

Emotions are Your Friends

Should you choose to study with Raphael, you will be in the company of a glorious Archangel of comfort, acceptance, and healing. Remember that the emotions are here as your friends. Do not shun them as lower, but rather honor them as you honor any creation of God—with gratitude and thanks for each and every sunrise and each and every nourishing meal. You can use the prayers in chapter 14 to contact the energy of Raphael and to invoke his presence. You may also try the meditations as given or create your own. Of all the methods, we most recommend that you study and practice the L.E.A.R.N. technique. It is a powerful way to assist you in keeping your heart center open to the spirit of life.

Whatever has been repressed must someday be expressed.

12

Expressing the Feeling is Important for Healing: The Powers, Purpose, and Process of Raphael

THE ARCHANGEL RAPHAEL is often pictured carrying a walking staff in his hand. The walking staff of Raphael symbolizes the need for the soul to continue onward with its divine journey as inspired by Spirit. After the energy of Michael has lifted the scales and illusions from your eyes, the attributes of Raphael assist you with healing the hurts that you are now allowing yourself to view. On this segment of your journey, you are accompanied by the Archangel Raphael who will help you revisit the experiences of the past made evident to you now by the Sword of Truth.

The main power of the energy stream emanating from this beautiful Archangel is the power of feeling. Without the assistance of Raphael, the trauma of revisiting old emotional wounds could send one into a destructive cycle of self-pity and retribution. And while all darkness was originally born of light, it is nevertheless possible to stay in the shadow longer than you may need to.

A Visit to the Doctor's Office

Have you ever felt that you could not connect with your feelings? Most of us have experienced this inability to connect with our feelings at one time or another. This lack of connection occurs because we become out of sync with our emotional self. We get out of sync with our emotional self by each act of suppression that becomes repression.

The following example illustrates how expressing your feelings is important for healing. Let's say that you have a stomach ache. It is not a normal stomachache that comes and then quickly goes away. This stomachache has lasted for two straight days. So you make an appointment with a doctor to see just what is happening inside you.

You arrive at the doctor's office a few minutes before your appointment. You sit in the waiting room. After a short time you are called into the examination room to see the doctor.

He asks you to sit on the exam table. Then he asks you a question, "What brings you here today?"

You respond, "I don't feel well."

Then he starts examining you. He touches your leg and asks, "Does it hurt here?" You say nothing.

He touches your arm and asks, "Well, does it hurt here?" Again you say nothing.

He feels your head and then your stomach while asking, "Does it hurt here or here?" Again you say nothing.

In each case above, you were unable or unwilling to express what you were feeling in that particular area of your body. The doctor had no way of knowing which part of you to treat! Just as expressing your sensations of physical ailments to your doctor in the outer world helps the physician diagnose and treat you, expressing your feelings generated by your experiences allows the inner doctor inside of you to heal your emotional wounds. Expressing our feelings helps us to focus on the areas that need to be healed. Without this expression, healing is virtually impossible.

The opposite of expression is repression. Repression causes us to become numb to our emotional self. This is similar to having a chronic ailment and denying that it affects you and makes you feel bad. It is easy over time for a small pain to be accepted as commonplace. We then forget that we can live without that pain. Healing comes by first admitting to the ailment and then expressing the pain. If we wait too long to admit to the problem when it is manageable, it can become an emergency situation.

Hints to Help You Remain
in Sync with Your Emotions

1. **Carry the Sword of Truth.** Without the symbolic Sword of Truth, you may not be able to admit or see the truth of yourself. You may condemn yourself as well.

2. **Use the prayers and invocations in chapter 14.** This will help you become more aware of the healing presence of Raphael.

3. **Practice the meditations on contacting Raphael.** They help to still the mind so that you can become aware of other thought streams and vibrations.

4. **Study and use the L.E.A.R.N. technique.** This technique was inspired by Raphael. Pay extra attention to performing the nightly review—the key component of the L.E.A.R.N. technique.

5. **Relax.** Breath In . . . Breath Out . . . and BE!

What is Healing?

Understanding healing can be a difficult task. If you define healing from a pure energy standpoint, it can be seen as the realignment of the energy centers of the body. When all energy centers are healed they work in harmony, which in itself brings to us a state of bliss and peace.

The process of expressing is a process that allows the energy centers to release repressed energy patterns. These repressed energy patterns act as gravitational forces upon the specific energy center they are associated with. While the energy is attempting to spin in a balanced manner within the center, it is constantly being acted upon by the gravitational forces of repressed and unprocessed energies.

When expression begins, a tremendous amount of energy can be released. The energy center may try to counteract this release by swinging wildly to and fro, attempting to find a balance point. This is why, when we start expressing our feelings, we may find that things appear to be getting worse, not better. This seeking of equilibrium within an energy center is normal and to be expected—especially after years of repression.

It is said that "time heals all wounds," and that eventually the emotional pain of an experience is deadened by the passage of time. But within that healing is an opportunity for growth. Don't ignore old experiences because they no longer seem to draw your attention. Valuable lessons lie hidden, waiting for us to uncover and examine them. Use the L.E.A.R.N. technique to process your experiences from the past and use it to process your daily experiences as well. This will help to keep the energy centers balanced and open to the spirit of life.

As we process more of our experiences from the past, we find that our way becomes clearer in the present. It is as if a fog of numbness lifts from around us. We had been shrouded in a fog of numbness that had kept our feelings hidden from ourselves. As the fog lifts, we can once again feel the pure energy of the emotions and see the road ahead.

Substitutes for Healing

When we hide our hearts, we disconnect and disassociate ourselves from our humanity. We no longer face life openly. We are afraid to honestly exchange energy with our spouses, partners, and children. Instead of honest communication, we may now find that we have substituted controllable activities (addictions) that supply us with a diversion that we call happiness. Thus repression has moved us to addiction and dependency.

Some common addictions and dependencies include:

- Abuse of non-prescription drugs,
- Abuse of alcohol,
- Overeating,
- Excessive shopping/buying,
- Religious fanaticism,
- Replacement of participation with watching (i.e., sports),
- Overworking—at home and at work, or
- Anything to excess.

If you can identify yourself in one or more of these addictions or dependencies, that's great! It's not great because of the addiction itself, rather it is great because you can admit that you, in fact, do have an issue or issues to deal with. You have taken a step away from repression by allowing yourself to view the truth. But do you honestly know and can you truly feel what the addiction or dependency is costing you—and what it will cost you if extended into your future?

If you cannot conceptualize the cost of this addiction, then try to think back to the time when this dependency was not yet formed. Try to remember when this activity first became a hiding place for you. Take a moment now to remember. What hurt or emotion do you recall feeling that led you to establish this hiding place for yourself? Take the experience that hurt you and attempt to process it by using the L.E.A.R.N. technique.

You may need to dig deep because your addiction serves a purpose in your life now. But you, and all those around you, will benefit if you can find a way to fulfill that purpose in a more healthy way. Within the experience of breaking an addiction lies the opportunity to extract pearls of wisdom by proper experiential processing. These new pearls of wisdom that you cultivate are integrated into the wisdom pool of your higher self.

Addictions are Symptoms of Repression

Why does Raphael want you to break these dependencies? Simply because each of them reduces your power to feel. A side effect of repression is that our power to feel is diminished. This is because we have inversely applied our power to feel by abusing the substances listed above, which in turn numbs our emotional energy centers to the full spectrum of emotional energy.

To add to the heartache, our addictions and dependencies can be difficult—if not deadly—to break. If you are addicted to physical substances, you may need professional help to solve your addiction. Seek help as appropriate—but also seek to remove your repression. You can resist your habitual tendencies toward repression by strengthening the power of feeling within you.

The dependency, as a substitute energy pattern, can never really replace the need it is attempting to fill. If it did then we would all be happy and content already—right? Addictions are substitutes for achieving the state of feeling wherein you can actually feel. This state of feeling is the state of living life open to life itself—to all of it. The addiction creates a false image of reality. We find this false image to be a pale reflection of the fullness of living with your energy centers open and spinning freely.

Ironically, we carry within us all of our repressions. The fact that we fail to express our feelings doesn't mean that we don't feel. These feelings are left to be processed later. Therefore, whatever has been repressed must eventually be expressed. Often it is in doing without that we come to appreciate what it means to do with! Complacency is seen therefore as the self unaware of its liabilities.

Remember that we use the power of feeling to process our experiences. This brings up the purposes of Raphael again: healing, wholeness, and acceptance. The following short exercise can help you uncover and process your repression. It is called the "Link" technique and is designed to demonstrate what it feels like to discover that you have been repressing rather then expressing your true feelings.

EXERCISE
The Link Technique

1. Take out a piece of paper.

2. Think of three significant people in your life.

3. Now, for each of the three people, write down three issues that you cannot talk about with them. This could be a love issue or an old grudge. When you are finished, you should have a total of nine issues.

4. Next, starting with the first significant person, take the first issue that you cannot talk with them about and write down three reasons why you cannot talk with them about it. Each reason must clarify the reason before it. Like a child who out of curiosity keeps asking his mother "Why? Why? Why?" Ask yourself "Why?" to each of the reasons that you write down in succession. Do this for the second and third issues for the first person.

5. Now repeat the step above for the second person, and then the third person.

6. **If you do this exercise with the seeing power inspired by Michael you will begin to uncover and face your repression.**

The act of facing repression is often enough to take the next step: to process your experiences in the area uncovered. Usually the repression is just the tip of an iceberg of emotions. Depending upon the amount of repression that has occurred, there could be even more expression required to cleanse and heal. The power of feeling can help you express. In fact, it is when you allow yourself to feel fully, that you cannot help but express—either that or you simply repress again.

In expressing your feelings, you may choose to compromise with the situations and people that you are involved with. In the past, you may have made "compromises" by simply shutting up and repressing your true feelings. This is a form of deception. As you learn to effectively express yourself, the compromises you make will come from a conscious state of awareness. As you become more honest with yourself and others, you may end up moving out of old relationships and situations.

Sometimes what we fear is what we desire. When you express your feelings you are living truth—the truth of yourself. We cannot force others to express themselves in the way we want them to. While you strive to express yourself clearly, others around you are expressing/repressing themselves as well. We must come to accept another person's choice to repress or express while accepting our own process as valid.

How to Resist Your Instinct to Repress

No one said this would be easy! Here are some tips to review if you feel you are not expressing your feelings. We usually know when we are repressing our feelings; this knowingness comes from that small still voice within us—our conscience.

1. **Remember that repressing is the opposite of expressing!** If you truly want to live a full, passionate, and loving life (here and now), remind yourself that expression is the process that you participate in by exercising your God-given power of feeling.

2. **Consider your commitment to growth.** If you have chosen the goal of angelic enlightenment, which is to integrate your self-segments, you obviously wish to succeed. Remember that you have chosen this goal of your own free will.

3. **Practice the techniques and meditations.** Try to use the L.E.A.R.N. technique anytime you feel the urge to repress by means of any of your chosen dependencies. Chapter 15 describes each step of the L.E.A.R.N. technique for you.

The four Archangels work together in harmony to guide you through their plan of healing. As Michael helps you to view truth through the power of seeing, the Archangel Raphael will help you heal with the power of feeling.

It is through the Archangel Raphael's power of feeling that we are given the opportunity to learn his process of expressing. After expressing our feelings we come to the states of acceptance, healing, and wholeness. This is the purpose of the energy stream emanating from Raphael.

If you think that you have nothing to heal,
it is quite possible that you are afraid to feel.

13

A Message from Raphael

The First Step to Feeling Better is to Feel!

As you take steps toward healing and wholeness, I ask you to remember that behind the pain that you are now brave enough to face is a love that has always been with you. With the help of Michael you are now facing your fears and uncovering the masks that you have worn for so long. I now ask you to view each experience of the past and the present without repressing your emotions.

Express those emotions: love, hate, anger, bliss. This is the human experience. The emotions are God-given. You do not need to heal your emotions! Your emotions are here to heal you.

Expressing your feeling is important for healing. Repression leads to implosion as the life force in your body system becomes twisted by the incomplete acceptance of the experience which generated the emotion. Many have wasted their precious existence by refusing to accept their experiences, good and bad. But I say to you, what choice do you have but to accept?

I, of myself, can do nothing to heal you. I do not heal with magic, nor do I heal with potions. I have no physical form, no body do I wear. All that I do is point to your heart; it is there that you must return. I will assist when asked but not unless requested. But when requested I will always assist. Yet it is you who must express the feelings that you have and it is you who must delve deeper to find the root where lies the seeds of all experiences.

Until you do you are living only a portion of your life. The lamp is lit, yet you close your eyes! I say unto you, "Open your eyes O man, and fear not the truth of thyself. Open your heart, O man, and feel the truth of yourself."

If you fail to express thyself, you will remain a stranger to the love that has eluded you for so long. If you choose to remain closed to the joyous spirit of love, you will remain hidden from yourself. Come, and I will show thee the way to thy heart.

Why is there suffering in the worlds in which you live? Of what divine purpose does it exist? The purpose of suffering is to help make you aware of something that requires your direct and immediate attention in order to first simply survive, and then to thrive in your life. For example, when you touch something hot with your hand, the pain you feel alerts you that you must move your hand quickly or you will incur more pain and suffering. The same is true with the emotions.

Emotions can be generated by physical experiences. For example, a volley of heated words exchanged during an argument can be just as painful as being burned from the heat of a physical fire. Once the pain is felt, and you are suffering, the first reaction is to stop the pain! This is very important and is usually what occurs. If it doesn't, a physical situation can turn deadly (i.e., keeping your hand in the fire).

But for many people, the fear of being rejected by others and the misunderstanding of the importance of expressing their emotions causes them to twist their emotional reactions by suppressing and denying them. This is especially likely for those who follow a spiritual path that has ignored the true purpose of human emotions and has denounced them as lower and negative in nature. In the example above, one would deny that their hand was burned and that they felt physical pain. As silly as that sounds, many people do the same in relation to their emotions.

What happens when one suppresses the emotions? I ask you to consider what happens when one suppresses the physical pain of his hand in the fire or suppresses anything, for that matter.

Eventually there is so much suppression that a breakdown, or rather a breakout, of the emotional energy must occur! Unfortunately, many times the breakout is in reality a *break-in;* the stress created by stuffing away the honest reactions to life around you can result in internal physical problems and illnesses. As this cycle compounds on itself, you now become frantic to find the reasons for the new physical pain, not seeing that it may have been partially caused by the stress of not handling your body's built-in emotional responses in an open, honest, and timely way.

There is ultimately no added value for you to extend your emotional suffering, for all mental anguish and emotional suffering is based on your own personal set of values and beliefs. Considering how you make choices based on whether a certain action will create more pain or bring more pleasure, it can be assumed that you feel and believe—based on your values and beliefs—that it is more painful to fully face the pain that is causing your suffering then it is to suffer itself! In other words, it is your choice.

Once you have the knowledge that your choices, with regard to emotional and mental anguish, are determined by your experiences (which were influenced by your values and beliefs) you can set about freeing yourself. You do not need to hold yourself in suffering, nor do you need to be in anguish for months or even years. Consider this: you can unleash the power of love from within your heart today. Love knows no favorites. It is the sweet nectar of inner peace that is our essence. But how can you unleash the love within?

There are many ways to deal with your emotions. These methods include: totally repressing them; forgiveness of others and ourselves for our choices that have hurt ourselves and others; and being totally honest with ourselves and others as to what we are experiencing and feeling at any given moment.

Under my guidance, Linda and Peter developed the Circle of Angelic Enlightenment to bring forth a technique known as the L.E.A.R.N. technique. It can help you process your emotions and the pain of an experience by expressing, for example, the anger, sadness, and remorse you may feel while moving toward the tenderness, joy, and love that lies underneath the hurt. Study this technique.

Make it a part of your daily life. I promise that I shall be here with you to assist you as you unseal the tenderness of your hidden heart of love.

The healing that you seek is not the healing of the body alone, but the return to the heart of God. I shall assist you in your healing. I am your friend and will be your guide should you ask me to walk with you on the pilgrimage through your past. As you move through your day, remember that the first way to feeling better is to allow yourself to feel!

May the love within you flower and heal the wounds of life and enliven you with divine energy and peace.

Everyone feels their pain.
Not everyone acknowledges their pain.

14

Prayers and Meditations to Contact the Archangel Raphael

A Prayer on Healing

Dear Raphael,

I pray to you to be with me as I strive to allow my heart to heal from the unresolved wounds of my past. Please send your healing energy as I move to heal my hurts daily, in truth and love. I promise to you that I will follow your guidance as I commit to healing all aspects of my being.

This I ask of you through the universal Christ energy, Amen.

MEDITATION

On Raphael's Presence

Take a seat in an easy chair or lie on a bed. Loosen any tight fitting clothes. Use the method you are best suited to for relaxation (such as deep breathing). This will help you focus inwardly. Make sure that you will not be disturbed for 15 to 30 minutes. After your mind has quieted and your body is relaxed, continue with the rest of the meditation.

Imagine that you are walking outside in the daylight. It is sunny and warm. There are only a few clouds in a blue sky. You are on a forest path. The trees are tall but you do not feel hemmed in. You can hear the sounds of birds and the rustle of the small forest animals as they scurry about.

You stop and sit by a small pond. You reach down and cup some water in your hands and drink. The coolness of the water refreshes you. As you look down at the water you see a reflection appear. It is the form of a man. You see that he is holding a walking staff in his hand.

You stand up and turn around. You are face to face with a beautiful being of light. Love is shining from his eyes. He extends a hand to you and tells you that he is the Archangel Raphael.

Imagine him in all his details. What is he wearing? What is the color of his hair? Look at his staff. What kind of wood is it made from? Are there carvings in the wood of the staff?

You notice a golden glow that emanates from around his whole being. He asks you if he can walk with you on your journey. What do you say to him?

Stay in this scene for as long as it feels comfortable to do so. Ask any questions of Raphael that you wish. Ask for his advice and help on your journey.

After a while thank him and slowly open your eyes. Relax and allow the healing presence of Raphael to wash over you. Consider what you have experienced during this meditation.

A Prayer on Wholeness

Dear Raphael,

My prayer on wholeness is to become more fully myself. To embrace each part of myself; my past, my present, and my future. I ask you to help me see the truth of my neighbors, my friends, and my challenges so that I may understand the design of the Creator. I commit that I will consider other viewpoints before speaking, and that I will respect other viewpoints when listening.

This I ask of you through the universal Christ energy, Amen.

MEDITATION

On Acceptance

Take a seat in an easy chair or lie on a bed. Loosen any tight fitting clothes. Use the method you are best suited to for relaxation (such as deep breathing). This will help you focus inwardly. Make sure that you will not be disturbed for 15 to 30 minutes. After your mind has quieted and your body is relaxed continue with the rest of the meditation.

Imagine that you are outside. It is just before sunrise. It is still dark. You are dressed in a relaxed fashion. It is warm. There is no breeze. You are comfortable. The light begins to change from black to shades of dark blue. The stars begin to fade slightly. After a few moments of enjoying the scenery, the sun begins to rise. You watch as the golden circle of light starts its ascent. The sky changes as streams of colored light extend as far as you can see.

After a short time the scene fades. You now become aware of the blazing brightness and heat of the noonday sun overhead. There are no shadows to be found; only light. There is no cold; only warmth. The brightness is startling at first but you become used to it. Everything is alive and responding to the energy rays from the sun.

This scene too fades, and there is a moment of blackness. You turn around to see the sun setting on the western horizon. As it sets you feel a sadness, but you are also excited. The stars and planets will soon fill the infinite night sky! You relax and accept the setting of the sun. You marvel at the beauty. You know that the sun will rise again. You let go and enjoy the moment.

Next there is complete blackness and you seem to be floating, suspended in space. All around you is space, but you are not afraid. A circle of light opens to your left. Within it forms an image of yourself as you are being born. You see your mother accept you into her arms and hold you close to her bosom. She wraps your little hand around her finger.

Directly in front of you, another circle of light appears. In it you see another image. This image is of yourself as you are today. You are smiling and see that you are very happy. In this image you see all the good and bad that has occurred in your life. You feel the sorrow and the joy within your heart. You accept being alive.

After a few moments, another circle of light opens to your right. Inside this circle you see yourself once again. This time you are preparing to leave this world. It is the end of the life cycle. You have made proper preparations with yourself and your loved ones. You have reviewed your life. As you begin to leave the body, an overall sense of well-being surrounds you.

As the sun rises, proceeds to its apex, and sets behind a curtain of stars so too do we, as living embodiments, rise up from the earth to form our life. As the elements that form our bodies are called back to the world, we ascend as ethereal matter into the stars of the spiritual worlds. We know that we will rise again, either in this world or another.

Relax. Ponder on life's cycles. Work with the concept of acceptance. Embrace all of the cycles, for to ignore and reject one, is to reject them all.

Open your eyes, take a deep breath, and look around. You are alive and well, and ready to live your life this day.

A Prayer on Acceptance

Dear Raphael,

I pray that I will have a conscious awareness of your presence. I ask that I may find the support I need so I can bring forth into my life an acceptance of the choices I have made. I will strive to hold and consider before I ignore or judge. As I live my life, I hope that my heart will be as your heart—pure and loving.

This I ask of you through the universal Christ energy, Amen.

When you cannot feel your feelings
then you are not in sync—not emotionally connected.

15

The L.E.A.R.N. Technique:
An Exercise with Raphael

THE L.E.A.R.N. TECHNIQUE was designed through the inspiration of the four Archangels. Although each Archangel's influence can be felt using this methodology, Raphael, the Archangel of healing, is the main proponent of the L.E.A.R.N. technique. This powerful technique combines multiple elements of angelic enlightenment and is the keystone technique of angelic enlightenment.

The L.E.A.R.N. technique is designed to gently integrate the emotional self. One of the most difficult self-segments to understand and integrate is that of the emotional self. Commonly misunderstood, the powerful feelings called emotions sway us to action or inaction. As emotional self-integration is accomplished, the conscious self and the basic self both benefit. A triune alignment of energy occurs that acts to unlock the heart center, bringing myriad blessings into light.

L.E.A.R.N. is an acronym. The word *learn* is appropriate as an acronym because we are here to experience and grow. *Learning* means to take our experiences in life, process them, and grow from the result of that processing. The letters of the L.E.A.R.N. acronym stand for the following:

L = Label
E = Express
A = Accept
R = Release
N = Nightly review

Refer to the *Discovering the Root Emotion* and the *Nightly Review* forms at the end of this chapter, (page 114 and 115) as you read the following pages. Use these forms in correlation with the steps of the L.E.A.R.N. technique. Blank forms are included in Appendix B so that you may make copies for your personal use.

Use the following steps when you are confused about the feelings you may have in a given situation. Pick a situation that puzzles or concerns you and summarize it on the *Discovering the Root Emotion* form in appendix B. A sample form is included in this chapter for your review. This example will help you to see how to use the form. After summarizing the situation, continue with the exercise.

1. Labeling Your Emotions

Understanding our emotions requires us to accurately label exactly what we are feeling. Believe it or not, many people have not been taught, nor do they remember, how to identify what they are feeling.

The first step is to identify your initial feelings (i.e., anger, rage, jealousy). Under step one of the *Discovering the Root Emotion* form, write down as many statements as you can that describe your feelings about the situation you are considering.

If you find that you are having difficulty identifying your feelings, try to remember that this first step is not about expressing the underlying emotion but only the surface or apparent emotion. For example, you know when you are angry—right? Or you know when you feel jealous. Write down those apparent feelings. We'll work on the root emotion later in the exercise.

Refer to chapter 28, "A Guide to the Emotions." There you will find some common (apparent) emotions with definitions. There are also many variant emotions that point back to the common emotion. Use the tables in chapter 28 if you are having difficulty identifying the apparent emotion. Once you identify the emotion and write your statements, you are ready for the next step of the technique.

2. Expressing What You are Feeling

We now move to the action of expressing the emotion that we have just labeled. Steps one and two can often occur simultaneously. Expression is sometimes done automatically with little supervision of the intellectual self. At other times, it is as if our conscious self is standing back and watching our emotional self act out (express) the emotion in question. At these times we can use the energy of the emotion to direct the self to go deeper to the root emotion in an effort to express with words and gestures a deeper part of our being. Expressing the root emotion is important to fully understand why we feel the emotion in the first place. For example, the emotion of anger is rarely felt alone, it is usually an extension of the emotion of sadness or fear.

Under step two of the *Discovering the Root Emotion* form, write down the feelings (i.e., pain, disappointment, hurt, rejection, fear) that are underneath the first layer of feeling that you identified in step one. Write down as many statements as you can that describe your feelings. Once again, you may wish to refer to the sample form in this chapter.

This is a most important step. If you fail to move deeper past the apparent layer you will not be able to gain the deepest wisdom of the experience. You have chosen to repress rather than express. This is not wrong, but it doesn't help you to process your experience in the present. There are even more steps to processing after expression. Try to allow yourself to feel. You may end up crying or feeling waves of emotional energy as you move deeper toward the source of your feelings. Move along deeper. Remember your love of truth and desire for growth.

After you have written down your feelings at this level, you are ready for the next step of the technique. If you cannot write anything in this step or feel that you haven't expressed yourself well, then you may want to wait until another time before proceeding to step three.

3. Accepting What You are Feeling

Acceptance means that we accept what we are feeling and do not attempt to re-define the feeling into a more agreeable emotion. For example, some people are taught that to feel anger is bad or negative. When they experience this emotion their intellectual self, powered by the basic self, will incorrectly label the emotion. This creates an unfortunate chain reaction built on the inability to accept the truth of our emotions. Acceptance is critical for honest self-examination and growth.

Under step three of the *Discovering the Root Emotion* form, write down the feelings underneath the pain and fear in step two (i.e., guilt, regret, ownership of your own feelings and the part you played in helping to create the situation). The sample form in this chapter will give you an idea of how to perform this step.

This step is essentially moving you deeper past the root emotion to the core of your being. You are extracting the kernel of wisdom from the experience. What happens next is the natural step of the integration of the wisdom into the wisdom pool of your higher self. This happens behind the scenes. Acceptance brings with it a calmness. It is like being in the eye of the storm. Tension is released and you are at peace with the experience. You are now ready for the next step.

4. Releasing the Emotion

The next stage is release. This does not mean to give up the experience you have had. Release means that, after you have identified (labeled) the emotion, expressed the root emotion (the truth of yourself), and accepted that you have indeed felt that emotion, you can then move on. For example, some people may label an emotion as anger, then express it to an individual or to themselves. They do accept that what they felt was truly anger but instead of releasing, they hold onto that energy stream. By holding onto the energy stream of anger, for example, the person can spiral into a destructive cycle.

If we find that we cannot, or will not, release the emotion it doesn't indicate that we are bad, it simply means that we haven't yet expressed the deeper levels of the emotion in question. Until we express the root emotion, we will not easily be able to release the experience. This may require us to revisit the experience at a later time when we have developed a greater endurance for self-examination.

Under step four of the *Discovering the Root Emotion* form, write down the feeling underneath the regret and guilt from step three (i.e., love, appreciation, forgiveness, and hopes for the future). Write down as many statements as you can that accurately describe your feelings. Once again, refer to the sample form in this chapter to see how this step works.

This completes the steps of the *Discovering the Root Emotion* form. Use this form to assist you in moving through the stages of processing your experiences. Eventually you may not need to use the form and that's ok. The steps of processing your experiences become a part of your outlook and a natural part of your life. The final step of the L.E.A.R.N. technique (nightly review) is used on a daily basis as explained below.

Nightly Review: Accelerate Your Growth and Learning

The last stage of the L.E.A.R.N. technique is an exercise called the *Nightly Review.* Each night, for a period of ten to thirty minutes, we take the time to review the events of the current day. We go through them in reverse order starting with right before bedtime all the way back to rising that morning. As we review the experiences of the day and the emotions generated by them, we take a moment with each to ask ourselves how we could have handled ourselves differently. How could we have labeled, expressed, accepted, and released our experiences with more honesty?

There are many events in the day. Some are minor, while others carry great significance for us. To help you process the major events of the day, you may wish to use the *Nightly Review* form. There are five steps on the form. Follow these five steps for each significant event of the day that you wish to process. Use a separate form for each significant event. Refer to the sample *Nightly Review* form included in this chapter. We've filled it out as an example for you to study on page 115.

Here are the five steps to follow on the form:

Step 1. Describe the event and what happened. In your own words, simply describe the physical event as it happened. Try to be as objective as you can. Do not write about your feelings—just the event itself.

Step 2. What are your main feelings about the event? Write down your feelings about what happened. Remember what you learned in the earlier parts of the L.E.A.R.N. technique and apply that knowledge to this step. In other words, try to write your feelings from the apparent emotion down to the root emotion.

Step 3. How did you handle the event, what did you do? Once again, objectively describe what actions you took during the event. Be honest.

Step 4. How would you change the way you handled the situation? Review what you wrote in steps 1, 2, and 3. Then write down how you would have preferred to handle the situation. Would you have chosen differently if you took the opportunity to feel the deeper levels of the experience before acting or speaking?

Step 5. Develop a plan to amend the situation. If you feel that the event requires a resolution of some kind, then decide what that will be and make a commitment to yourself to carry it out. This does not mean that you must always talk with other people involved in the event. Your plan for amending the situation should take into consideration the feelings of others.

Remember that this is not a time to hammer ourselves, rather it is an opportunity to use the God-given faculty of the imagination to re-live and re-write key moments of our day. This extends the learning potential of our daily experience. The nightly review is in itself a powerful tool for self-understanding and growth. By using these steps you create an ever-increasing circle of growth, built from one day to the next.

The L.E.A.R.N. technique inspired by Archangel Raphael will assist you in living your life to the fullest. Practice it with care, and you will see results in your life. You will feel the joy of living again. Your heart will be aflame with love and you will find that which you seek.

You do not need to heal your emotions!
Your emotions are here to heal you.

The L.E.A.R.N. Technique

Discovering the Root Emotion

Date: __1-25-98__   Time: __2:00 pm.__

Describe what happened: I was attending the wake of a neighbor who had recently passed away. She had been much loved by the whole community. As we said our farewells to her, I mentioned how she had sometimes given me Christmas gifts, even though I wasn't an immediate relative of hers. My sister + mom responded by saying, "I wonder why she gave you gifts — she never gave us any." Then my mom said, "I think she just gave you gifts because you happened to be around when she was giving gifts to your other sister."

1. Label: Identify your initial feelings (anger, rage, jealousy, etc.) and write down as many statements as you can that describe these feelings.

Anger → I felt angry because they didn't acknowledge the kindness and generosity of this lady.

Blocked → My energy felt blocked because of their reaction to my comment.

Jealousy → Old feelings of sibling rivalry came up because my mom's comment seemed to imply that my sister was worthy of receiving gifts + somehow I wasn't.

2. Express: Write down the feelings (pain, disappointment, hurt, rejection, fear, etc.) that are underneath the first layer of feeling that you identified in step 1.

Hurt → I felt hurt and misunderstood since their comments seemed to de-value the neighbor's generosity as well as de-valuing my "worthiness" in being the recipient of these gifts.

Disappointed + Frustrated → because our conversation was unclear + painful instead of positive and affirming.

Insecurity + fear → I was afraid they were right. Perhaps this lady really didn't like me and had only given me the gifts because I happened to be there and she didn't want me to feel

3. Accept: Write down the feelings underneath the pain and fear in step 2 (guilt, left out, regret, ownership of your own feelings and the part you played in helping to create the situation).

Regret and Sadness → I regreted the fact that our conversation was unclear and un-supportive of each other. I wished that I had phrased my comment differently and that I had simply commented on her generosity and my appreciation for her generosity. Instead, my comment caused them to wonder why she hadn't given them any gifts (it had aroused their own insecurities) and thus they did not acknowledge her generosity or the possibility that she had given me the gifts because she simply

4. Release: Write down the feeling underneath the regret and guilt from step 3 "liked" me. (love, appreciation, forgiveness, and hopes for the future).

Love → I realized how much I value the love and approval of others, especially my family.

Forgiveness → I am given the opportunity to forgive myself for not communicating clearly my feelings and my reactions to their comments. I forgive them as I realize their comments reflected their own insecurities — and not an attack upon me.

Hopes for the future → I hope that as I learn to phrase my comments lovingly and honestly then others can also come from a point of truth and love within themselves. I hope that we can learn to communicate with one another in loving and supportive ways — from a point of truth rather than insecurity.

The L.E.A.R.N. Technique
Nightly Review

Date: 1-25-98   Time: 10:00 p.m.

1. **Describe the event and what happened.** I was attending the wake of a neighbor who had recently passed away. She had been much loved by the whole community. As we said our farewells to her, I mentioned how she had sometimes given me Christmas gifts, even though I wasn't an immediate relative of hers. My sister + mom responded by saying, "I wonder why she gave you gifts — she never gave us any." Then my mom said, "I think she just gave you gifts because you happened to be around when she was giving gifts to your other sister."

2. **What are your main feelings about the event?** I felt anger, hurt, sadness and jealousy. I felt de-valued. I felt "blocked," frustrated, and misunderstood. I had been trying to share a positive memory of this lady, at her wake, instead of affirming my comment + the lady's generosity; they responded from a point of their own insecurities.

3. **How did you handle the event, what did you do?** I reacted from a point of anger and hurt. I "threw" a question back at my mom to the effect of, "Well then, why didn't she (the neighbor) give gifts to <u>every one</u> who happened to be present?"

4. **How would you change the way you handled the situation?** I would communicate more clearly. First, I would simply say how much I appreciated the generosity and kindness of this lady. I would mention my gratitude for the gifts she gave me at Christmas time. Thus, these comments would not be as likely to provoke feelings of insecurity within my sister + mother.

5. **Develop a plan to amend the situation.** I will discuss my feelings honestly as they arise in each situation. I will try to communicate clearly and kindly, from a point of truth and love.

   Instead of reacting in anger (by "throwing" the question back at my mom) I will instead explain my feelings and reactions as honestly as I can in each moment. For example, I will begin with, "It hurts my feelings when..."

Section 4

The Archangel Gabriel

And the angel answering said unto him,
"I am Gabriel, that stand in the presence of God;
and I was sent to speak unto thee,
and to bring thee these good tidings."

—Luke 1:19

16

Gabriel: The Archangel of Strength and Commitment

THE THIRD ARCHANGEL is Saint Gabriel. Gabriel is most well known from the numerous paintings of the Annunciation. Sometimes adorned in flowing robes with a scepter in his hand, and at other times as a female Angel with a flower in her hand, Gabriel is shown announcing to the Virgin Mary that she is to be the mother of the Christ.

The scepter or flower is a symbol of the divine task, or mission from God as delivered by Gabriel. Mother Mary would need to rely on the Godly attributes of strength, persistence, and commitment in order to guide the young Christ through to adulthood and his divine mission.

The essence of this part of your journey is to build the attributes of strength, commitment, and persistence as you learn to use your power to act in order to define and accomplish your divine life's mission. The beneficial results that have graced your life since following the guidance of Michael and Raphael have prepared you for Gabriel's dynamic presence.

Gabriel makes his presence known to you after you have chosen to exercise the power of seeing and the power of feeling. Michael has taught you how to uncover and understand the current situations of your life through this seeing power—the ability to honestly view the part you play in fashioning your experiences. Raphael has taught you how to process your emotions. By using the power of feeling you have been able to clear hidden blockages within your energy centers.

The Ninety-Pound Weakling

To illustrate the way Michael and Raphael have prepared you for the guidance and challenges of Gabriel, we've chosen to review the old cartoon of the ninety-pound weakling.

As you may recall, this story centers around a frail young man about eighteen years of age. It is set on a beach. The day is hot and sunny. The ninety-pound weakling comes across an arrogant, muscle-bound bully. The bully essentially beats up and embarrasses the ninety-pound weakling in front of everyone on the beach, including a beautiful blonde in a bikini.

The ninety-pound weakling goes home and looks at himself in the mirror. This represents our conscious self willing to look at the truth of our lives in the present state—good and bad. The weakling is honest with himself. He admits that he doesn't have large muscles. In fact, it looks as if he has hardly any muscles at all. He has ignored his body. In a similar way, when the energy of Michael is infused and operating within us, we choose to be honest with ourselves. We come to admit that we have ignored vital areas in our lives—that our lives are not what we wished them to be.

The weakling goes on to process his feelings of embarrassment about the incident. This is an important step, since the weakling could have simply repressed his feelings by rationalizing that the bully was just a jerk. He could have told himself that his body was in good physical shape already. If he had repressed his feelings of embarrassment and hurt, then the energy of the emotion would have been unavailable to him. Although the energy of repressed emotions remains in the "repression pressure cooker" for later extraction, the weakling could have benefited immediately by processing the emotion in the present. The released emotional energy could have been used to drill deeper to the root cause of the emotion so that wisdom could be extracted and the lesson learned.

In the story, the weakling chose to express his emotions directly. He did this to himself while looking into the mirror. He allowed himself to feel the embarrassment and hurt which in turn gave him the energy to change. This is the same as when we look into the mirror of truth and decide to express rather than repress our emotions. We learn and grow. The lessons learned in the present help us to define the direction we wish to move in the future.

Taking the Energy and Creating Change

Our weakling did not stop with the understanding and expression that came from his seeing and feeling powers. He took the next step and decided the course that he wanted his life to take. He was going to change the state of his body. In order to accomplish this physical change he decided to eat properly and exercise regularly.

Over a period of several weeks, he followed his plan diligently. Each day he took in the proper nourishment from the earth and transformed it into muscles and tendons. Along with the intake of food, he increased his activity in the form of running and lifting weights. In this way, he exercised the power of acting by taking energy and rearranging its form and location. His body responded. He accomplished his goal and in the process he gained in the attributes of strength, commitment, and persistence.

In the same way as this weakling, we, as the conscious self, make a plan—a blueprint for change. This change brings us experiences that we desire. Our blueprint could consist of small tasks or major tasks such as determining our life's mission and carrying it out (much the same way as the weakling did with his body).

As we choose to act, we move energy. We take the energy in by processing our experiences, then we fashion it into the building blocks and forms that we use to bring our respective blueprints into manifestation. We have exercised our power of acting, which results in the accomplishment of our goals and an increase of our strength. This increase has an exponential effect—it strengthens us internally so that we face all of life with a new awareness.

The more we understand about the overall process of life, the more we choose to open our hearts to life's energy. The more we open our hearts to life's energy, the more building blocks we have available to create with! This is the purpose of Gabriel.

Proper Use of the New Strength

Our ninety-pound weakling returned to the beach after he had accomplished his physical changes. On that day, the bully, not able to appreciate the changes in the weakling, again tried to abuse the situation. The weakling promptly defended himself by knocking the bully to the ground. The blond in the bikini was now on the weakling's arm while the bully was given the opportunity to learn and grow as a result.

The new strength of the weakling could have been misused. He could have chosen to go to the beach with the intentions of hurting and punishing the bully. He could have held hatred in his heart. It is vital that we understand the desire that lies behind our choice to change, act, and accomplish. Is it to destroy, hurt, or glorify our ego-centric-self? If the self-truth and self-honesty that you give yourself is pure, then you can assume that your motivations are also pure—to better yourself in some way. This means to better ourselves in a way that is not at the expense of others.

Ways to Increase Your Strength

Here are some tips that can help you move the energy around you by using your power to act:

1. **Look into the mirror of truth.** See yourself in the mirror of truth. Without viewing yourself honestly—as you know you should—increasing your strength to change may never come. When we exercise our power to act (to create change) the attribute of strength increases within us.

2. **Fully process your experiences.** Much the same as consuming the kernel provides our bodies with the most nutritious part of grain, proper and full processing of our experiences supplies us with pure energy. We can use that energy to transform our lives.

3. **Set small goals and stick to them.** It does no good to establish wild goals such as exercising three hours a night, seven days a week. We set ourselves up for failure and exhaustion. Set small goals. For example, exercise twenty minutes each day, three days a week. In this way, we allow ourselves to build our strength over time. Each success helps us build future successes.

What to Watch Out for as You Gain Strength

The following are some items that you may encounter as you increase your strength and power by exercising your ability to act:

1. **Arrogance**: If, as you gain strength, you start to feel emotions of superiority—stop and find the source of those emotions. When we feel the fear-based emotions (see chapter 28), it is time to use the L.E.A.R.N. technique of Raphael. Remember, the process of life is ongoing. We keep learning all the time. Increasing your strength will bring new awareness and experience to you—providing new challenges.

2. **Vanity:** During your association with Gabriel, strive to clearly see the part you play in the universal plan of God. Vanity points to areas that are seeking your attention. Take care to not repress this feeling. Remember, you feel what you feel. Your feelings are clues to follow. Once again, use the L.E.A.R.N. technique to explore the origin of the vanity. An exploration of vanity will lead to hidden insecurities.

3. **Self-Limiting Patterns and Beliefs:** In defining your mission and setting steps toward that accomplishment, avoid patterns and beliefs that limit your action toward that goal. While acknowledging your desire to not harm others in word or action, you need to allow yourself to act in areas that you are unaccustomed to. If this were not so you would have already reached your goal. For example, if you are trying to become more assertive in your work environment, take care that you do not actually become aggressive.

The Divine Dispatch of Gabriel

After we are awakened by the Sword of Truth of Michael, and have completed the journey of healing the emotional self with Raphael, the soul self and the conscious self are now the purified vessel of Spirit and are ready to accept the divine mission—our life's mission—in a greater completeness than ever before. The presence of Gabriel comes to us to announce that we are dispatched to begin our mission and to assist us along the way.

The purpose of the energy stream emanating from this powerful Archangel of God is to assist with the flowering of the Godly attributes of strength, persistence, and commitment within each of us. This is symbolized by Mary, as the divine feminine principle, being told that she was to be the mother of the Son of God. Mary represents the creative principle within each of us that has the power to give birth and manifest a new life into this world.

The scepter of Gabriel represents God's divine energy dispatched to Mary to give birth (bring into manifestation) a part of God, onto this earth. The communication between Gabriel and Mary symbolizes our acceptance of our life's mission. Our life's mission is our soul's purpose and is directed by the soul self through the Holy Spirit.

The birth of the Christ represents the bringing forth from our selves the commitment to the divine task that our soul has decided to undertake.

Most fortunate are those visited by the power of Gabriel. This means that one has usually accepted the Sword of Truth, completed the majority of the journey of healing the old emotional wounds, and is now ready to accept their life's mission free of the heart-covering masks and unresolved tensions of unvisited and unforgiven wounds. With the strength of the Archangel Gabriel, we are commissioned to begin that mission without delay!

The more we open our hearts to life's energy,
the more building blocks we have available to create even more!

17

Defining Your Life's Mission: The Powers, Purpose, and Process of Gabriel

PERHAPS SOME OF the most difficult questions to answer in life are "Why are we here?" "What is the purpose of life?" and "What is our individual purpose of being—our life's mission?" The Archangel Gabriel comes to us to offer us the choice to commit ourselves to action in accomplishing our life's mission. It is up to each of us, as the conscious self, to use the tools around us in order to open up to the wisdom of the higher self and the direction of the soul self.

By opening up to the soul self, we can re-connect with the inner knowledge of soul's pattern and purpose for this lifetime. When we catch a glimpse of our soul, chords of remembrance are struck within us. It is then that the image or impressions from the soul remind us of our purpose on earth as well as our mission.

Gabriel's Main Power

The main power of the energy stream emanating from Gabriel is that of the power of acting. The scepter is a symbol of the action of the divine will and the individual soul's purpose in this life. The offering of the scepter is actually symbolic. It represents the decision of the conscious self to accept or decline the dispatch of the soul self—to create, manifest, and carry through with soul's pattern and purpose.

By the power of acting, we are not referring to acting as if on a movie screen. The power to act is the ability to move energy in ways that adjust the forms and substances in the earth worlds. This rearranging is done for experience and learning. All of us on earth are interconnected to each other. A vast spiritual connection exists as we individually and collectively expand in consciousness.

An open mind is essential in allowing ourselves to expand into the roles needed to carry out our life's mission. It is also essential that we allow others to expand into their roles and missions as well. While we may not understand their choices, we should strive to respect them as beings of light and love living in the same human condition as we.

What is Your Life's Mission?

How can you act to accomplish your life's mission before you know what it is? Each experience holds a key. First, use what you have learned with Michael and Raphael. If you apply the lessons learned with them, you will increase your ability to accurately see your purpose from the soul viewpoint. Alternatively, misapplication or non-application of what you have learned may decrease your ability to act in constructive ways toward your goals.

If you are applying the lessons of Michael and Raphael in your life and you still do not have an awareness of your life's mission, you can try the following short exercise. It can help you to focus on connecting to the soul self in order to uncover your mission. Do not become frantic about uncovering your mission. Many times you are already on the right track. You are accumulating knowledge and preparing yourself right now! Enjoy the moment and the process. Remember, life is a process—not a result.

What's Your Line? Defining Your Life's Mission.

Do you recall the old game show "What's My Line?" On the program, a panel of celebrities wearing blindfolds would ask a series of questions of an unknown personality. The goal of the game was to guess the unknown person's profession. In this exercise, you are a celebrity on the panel and your soul self is the unknown personality.

Defining Your Life's Mission

Close your eyes and relax. Take a few minutes to clear your mind. After a short time, begin to imagine that you are sitting blindfolded in a chair. You hear the voice of a moderator announce the mystery guest as your soul self. Your soul self is dressed in the fashion of your unknown life's mission.

While you cannot see your soul self because you are blindfolded, you can still feel its presence. It is a presence that reassures you and makes you feel warm inside. You are very relaxed now.

Next the moderator says to you: "Ok, you know how the game goes. You get to ask ten yes/no type questions that relate to our mystery guest's occupation. After you ask the question, I will answer in the affirmative or the negative. Any time that you feel you know what the mystery guest's life's mission is, just ask and I'll tell you if you are correct or not. If you are not correct, the game is over and you'll have to play again later. At the end of the ten questions you also get one guess as to the mystery guest's occupation. Now begin with your questions."

As you sit in the chair, blindfolded, ask up to ten questions of the moderator. These questions must be phrased in such a way as to elicit a yes or no response from the moderator. Tailor your questions around a mission that you may feel attracted to. After you ask the question, listen for the moderator's response. It should be a yes or no. Each answer from the moderator should help you tailor your next question (the moderator is your intuitive self).

At the end of ten questions, or anytime you feel like you know the life's mission as shown by the soul self, tell the moderator. Listen again for his answer. If you are right, remove your blindfold to view your soul self. If you are wrong, try playing the game again later.

This simple exercise is a fun way to contact your soul self and to open your conscious self to the knowledge that lies within you.

The Process of Accomplishment

Our ability to act is not a denial of the fact that our bodies will someday die and that we shall leave this arena of action. Many leaders throughout history have applied their power—their ability to act—as a means to achieve immortality on earth. There is no immortality on earth for, as nature dictates, the stream of divine energy is always moving through the phases of creation, maintenance, and dissolution. Energy is the spiritual essence of forms and substances. It is rearranged so that we may have various experiences for learning and growth.

Our power to act is in itself divine because it emulates the Creator. In the process of creation we act to make a form for spirit to fill. Therefore, it is important to learn the lessons of Saint Michael and Saint Raphael. If we do not, then we may manifest a form that brings misery and pain to ourselves and to the people around us. Case in point are military dictators from the past who used their power to quench their desires, regardless of the cost in human suffering.

Remember that any act which disrespects life and the commitments we have made is an act which is made from an ill-balanced ego. Many on earth wish to work from a realm of non-interference and this, in theory, is good. But left unchecked, atrocities become commonplace and we become numb to the loss of our own innocence. Often, to add to the heartache, these atrocities are done for the sake of expediency, and we support them because we wish to have the same freedom should we need to commit these acts ourselves.

Therefore, it is not enough that we learn how to harness the power to act from studying with Gabriel; we must go the full distance and incorporate all the elements of each of the four Archangels. Without the seeing power of Michael, we act in the dark, unaware of the forces that have fashioned our conditioning. Without the feeling power of Raphael, we act out of skewed energy patterns created from years of repressing our emotions. And as you shall learn later, without the power of being that Archangel Uriel brings, we act out of a desire to conquer life and death.

So when we look at accomplishment, we see that the forms we construct for spirit to fill can originate from evil or good intentions. Spirit, like water, will fill the container constructed for it. Take the time to make sure that your accomplishments will be for the good of yourself and for the good of the whole.

For the Good of the Whole

This exercise is intended to help you to view the results of your accomplishments on earth *before* they are manifested and filled with the energy of spirit. This will help you objectively decide whether or not you should act in a certain area to accomplish a particular goal. After using this exercise you may decide to change a goal, delete it, or keep it unchanged. The purpose of this exercise is not to discourage you, but to empower you by helping you apply what you have learned so far.

E X E R C I S E

Evaluating Goals

First, as in most exercises, calm yourself. Do this by your favored method. It is good to be in an area where you will not be disturbed. This exercise should take only 5 to 10 minutes to accomplish.

Close your eyes if you have not already done so. Next, imagine your goal. See what it is that you are desiring to accomplish. Even though it may not be a physical building, it still is a form that energy must fill in order for it to exist on earth. You may, for example, see yourself as a healer using hands-on healing techniques with your patients. Picture yourself in your home office or wherever your imagination places you.

From this point of acting look backward at how you got to this place in your imagination. Did you study under various teachers? Whom did you have to interact with to accomplish this goal? How did you interact with them? Allow yourself to see yourself in different scenes. Each scene should show a step or steps that helped you accomplish the goal.

Pause for a few moments to process those scenes. Feel the feelings and view the motivations.

Now jump back to the scene of viewing your accomplishment. From this point, move day-to-day, month-to-month, and then year-to-year into the future. Watch scenes unfold between yourself and personalities you may know now and those you will meet. How is your accomplishment and your acting affecting other people? How is it affecting you? Do you see good things occurring? How are you feeling about the effects of your accomplishment?

Next jump back into the present moment with your eyes still closed. Imagine that the act and the accomplishment were never completed in this lifetime. Wait a few moments. Now how do you feel knowing that this particular goal was never reached? Does it bother you? If so, why? If not, then why doesn't it?

Do this for a short time. Gently open your eyes.

Try this exercise upon your chosen life's mission. If you are not aware of your life's mission, then try it on the different ideas you may have about your life's mission. Finally, you can also try this exercise on any goal you may have, at work and at home.

The Attributes of Strength, Persistence, and Commitment

Through exercising our power to act we have followed through with the process of Gabriel, which is to accomplish. As a result of the interplay between acting and accomplishing we have gained in strength, persistence, and commitment.

Strength

Bit by bit, as you have taken steps toward your goal, you have gained in strength. What were once seen as insurmountable obstacles to your goals are now seen as challenges. It is as if the high jump bar went from seven feet to three feet. The more you act, the stronger you become over time. With this strength must come responsibility. The incorrect application of our strength can hurt ourselves and others.

Persistence

Accomplishment leads to an awareness of the attribute of persistence. You learn to develop insight into situations. The challenges you face are made easier because you use your insight to find ways to accomplish your goal. When faced with a problem, you have found that you persist in finding a solution. If we begin to act toward accomplishing our goals and fail to employ persistence, we will give up in the early stages.

Commitment

You have developed strength and persistence, but without commitment, which is the choice to follow through until the end, your goals will probably never be reached. This commitment varies with the goal. Realizing that we, on earth, are constrained by time and space, we must choose to commit or allocate our resources to a limited number of goals. Without commitment you may lose focus and veer off from your goal. If you have attained your goal through accomplishment, you have shown a degree of commitment and understand this divine attribute.

Taking the Scepter

Gabriel offers you the scepter of divine dispatch. If you choose to take it, you begin the process of manifesting your life's mission. Through the exercises given, you can uncover and define your mission and take steps to accomplish it. Remember that accepting the scepter requires utmost respect for life, for ourselves, and for all others.

As you begin this process under the Archangel Gabriel, you will soon become aware of the presence of Uriel. As you shall learn, Uriel is the Archangel of love, beauty, and awareness. Uriel comes to work closely with you after you have accepted the scepter from Gabriel. He will help you to remember that accomplishing, in itself, is not the goal.

The goal in accomplishing your life's mission is to fulfill the soul's pattern and purpose. It is not to wield your power over others, but rather it is to use your power to manifest more and more divine love in your life. The soul, in itself, is good. We embrace the hurt parts of ourselves and accept the good and bad in the world. We are not here to condemn nor to tell others how to live nor what to do. As it is, we are here on earth and our duty is to honor and respect all life. We must find and accomplish our purpose within that framework.

The ability to act is enhanced by following the powerful technique inspired by the Archangel Gabriel called Creating Change. The Creating Change technique is explained in chapter 20. This technique can help you break old patterns and propel you into action. You can use it to manifest your life's mission and bring desired results into actuality.

The Archangel Gabriel can help you integrate your experiences so that you can take action to accomplish your life's mission. Remember to call upon him when you are in doubt and are unable to continue. His divine guidance is a blessing to those who become aware of his presence.

Reclaim your spiritual heritage.

18

A Message from Gabriel

The Transmutation of Energy

The roles you play on earth are classifications that describe how you relate to other individuals and forms. Each role you play comes with its areas of responsibilities as well as benefits. Each role also allows you to learn, share, and grow in different ways. For example, the role of a father toward his child is different than that of the man toward the wife or vice-versa.

You must remember not to get your roles confused. Many failing marriages will find one or both of the spouses relating to their children and each other in mixed roles—very often requiring the child to be the adult and to take sides in the disputes. You must avoid this mixture of roles in order to keep yourselves in balance and to help those around you maintain a state of consistency and security.

I come to you now to talk to you about energy. The One Energy. The God energy. The essence of all creation. This energy has never been created, it has never been destroyed. It is only changing—ever changing. This change is apparent through your experience of forms and substances in the worlds of energy, matter, space, and time. This One Energy is, has always been, and shall always be. The world is without end, for the energy that creates the world shall never dissipate nor vanish.

I come to you now to dispatch upon you the divine energy in a form that you can accept. I ask you to open up to the divine energy that is contained within the source of your own being. Open up to the soul self, the wisdom of the higher self, the clues of the emotional self, and the urgings of the basic self.

Through this cleansing process you will begin to see the truth of your choices and why you made them. This truth promotes the healing of your scarred and wounded child's heart. As the painful scars dissolve in the water of the Holy Spirit, you are now ready to define, begin, carry out, and complete your soul's purpose—your mission for this lifetime.

Your purpose as the conscious self is twofold. First is to keep yourself open to the divine spirit—the love current within your heart. Second is to understand the soul's purpose as it relates to your life's mission.

My purpose is to show you how to create change in your life. It is to show you how to take the knowledge that you have gathered, coupled with the healing that has occurred, and use the wisdom gained to move forward: to motivate yourself, to uncover, to discover, to implement, and to act and accomplish within this world.

Your world is a world of spirit and yet it is also a world of forms and substances that move and breathe and live and act. Your creation is a form of acting and as you accomplish you learn. There is a balance between being and acting. The energy of change consists of both being and acting.

As I once dispatched God's message to the Virgin Mary, so too do I now dispatch unto you your divine mission. The Virgin Mary received me in the purity of her heart. So too have you, who have worked and struggled to cleanse yourself with the water of life and to heal your hurts of the past, now come to the level of purity that is needed to accept and carry out your divine purpose and mission.

Until then, one may spin in despondency, depression, and anger, repeatedly trying to work through the energies of these emotions and to deal with the pain and suffering in the world. There is nothing wrong, or bad, or negative about this struggling, for it is a part of the human experience. But when you have the knowledge and choose *not* to apply it, you have lit a lamp and yet closed your eyes to create darkness.

The purity of Mary is the purity within you. It is the purity within all creations of God. It is concurrent with the central alignment of all the self-segments reacting in harmony with the Holy Spirit. It is in the duality of the world that you learn about alignment—for if there were no misalignment, there could be no concept of alignment.

I come to show you an example of strength. When you are down and unable to continue, look to me to gain inspiration in order to renew yourself. Draw deep from the well of strength within the soul self and allow the energy of healing to move through all the centers of your bodies.

I come to show you an example of persistence. No matter how hard your road becomes as you move toward accomplishing and creating, look to my example and do not give up. Always move toward your goal. The mountain is far away, but never a step closer until you begin your journey.

I come to show you an example of commitment. Commitment begins with the joining of hands, the clasping of arms, and the choice to walk the fields together as we plow and plant the seeds of creation unto the earth.

Remember to take time for yourself—to renew and recharge. Creating change is not a non-stop process. You must find your individual state of balance where you act and then be. This ebb and flow is natural and varies from individual to individual. The rest periods are as important as the active periods.

All life on earth consists of the transmutation of energy. All beings shape and move energy. The musician takes his energy and transmutes it through the body of his instrument, which in turn moves the energy of the atoms in the atmosphere creating sound. Each and every occupation in your world consists of changing forms and substances from one state to another or relocating forms and substances from one locale to another.

Manifestation is nothing more that a modification of the energy patterns available to bring change to forms. Destruction is the breakdown of a form. Creation is the manifestation of a form. All is One energy, always, forever, and never-ending.

Energy is like water, it conforms to the container you manifest for it. In some aspects, creation simply consists of the individual constructing a form within the matter substance that the spiritual energy fills. Energy is like water in the way that it is displaced by you as you move through a pool. Every movement you make while in a pool moves the water around you as every choice you make in your life moves the spiritual energy around you. Energy is constantly being moved, manipulated, and transmuted. In your rest periods, your body is moving energy from one form to another. There are no true static states. Your bodies are microcosms of the universes of God.

You are born from the dust of the earth. Your body is fashioned from the matter composed of the energy of God. Your nourishment is consumed and the energy is transmuted into a form that can sustain you. When you die your body will return to the earth. Energy rearranged in form to be used again, and again, as the building blocks of other forms, substances, and bodies—as vehicles for spirit. Those who are afraid to create change are afraid of themselves. Will their fear stop the death of their body?

Those who accept the divine dispatch of the Lord, as did Mary, accept themselves in the purity of the essence of the Creator. We are not compelled to accept this mission, nor are we forced to change in any way. It is always our free will and right to choose our course of action. When confronted with a choice, strive to uncover and know your motivations—understand why you choose the way you do.

I come to you now and will be with you when called upon. If you choose to accept my guidance, I will gladly and lovingly provide it for you. I will help by being an example of strength, persistence, and commitment to you as you define and manifest your life's mission.

This I commit to you in the spirit of strength through the universal Christ energy of the Creator.

It is always our free will and right to choose our course of action.

19

Prayers and Meditations to Contact the Archangel Gabriel

A Prayer on Strength

Dear Gabriel,
I pray to you to assist me as I develop the strength to carry out my life's mission. Please send your strengthening energy to help me to live life with courage and love for myself and all humanity. With your guidance I will strive to fulfill my purpose and assist others on their journey.
This I ask of you through the universal Christ energy, Amen.

MEDITATION
On Gabriel's Presence

Take a seat in an easy chair or lie on a bed. Loosen any tight fitting clothes. Use the method you are best suited to for relaxation (such as deep breathing). This will help you focus inwardly. Make sure that you will not be disturbed for 15 to 30 minutes. After your mind has quieted and your body is relaxed, continue with the rest of the meditation.

Imagine that you are in a garden. It is late afternoon and you are alone. You hear the sounds of nature. Birds are singing softly in trees which surround the garden. In the distance you hear the ripple of a stream. The stream is somewhere behind the trees. The grass is soft beneath your bare feet. The sun caresses you in a warm embrace.

You wander through the garden, stopping to appreciate each flowering bush and shrub. To your left is a beautiful rose bush. The fragrance of the rose bush draws you close. You approach the bush and breathe in the soothing scents. There is a stone bench next to the rose bush. You sit on the bench. It faces the entrance of the garden. You look around and sense that someone is near, someone you have known for a long time but have not seen in a great while.

After waiting a few more moments you see a robed figure appear from out of the forest and walk towards you. He is Gabriel. He is resplendent in his attire and regal in his appearance. Love radiates from all around him. You heart races as he approaches. He does not speak.

You want to stand as he approaches, but instead you fall to your knees as the awesome power of Gabriel enters and flows throughout your being. He takes your hand and leads you back to the stone bench where you sit again. Gabriel turns to the rose bush and gently plucks a white rose from a limb. He turns back to you and offers you the rose in his outstretched hand. You look into his eyes and then into your heart. You must decide if you are ready to accept your life's mission and to carry it out.

Take a moment now to feel the scene. Do you decide to take the rose? Ask Gabriel anything you wish to. Listen to his answers. Flow with this scene for a few minutes, moving where it may take you. When you are done, bid farewell to Gabriel and slowly open your eyes. Ground yourself to your surroundings. Take a few minutes to consider what you have experienced during this meditation.

A Prayer on Persistence

Dear Gabriel,

Please be with me as I work towards a full integration of the self. I promise to carry out the responsibilities I have chosen to accept for myself, my loved ones, and those for whom I work. Send me your energy as I continue to manifest my life's purpose. I will assist those less fortunate than I, as well as all who may ask for my help.

This I ask of you through the universal Christ energy, Amen.

MEDITATION

On Strength

Take a seat in an easy chair or lie on a bed. Loosen any tight fitting clothes. Use the method you are best suited to for relaxation (such as deep breathing). This will help you focus inwardly. Make sure that you will not be disturbed for 15 to 30 minutes. After your mind has quieted and your body is relaxed, continue with the rest of the meditation.

Imagine that it is afternoon. You are on your farmland outside of your house. The sun is shining. It is hot. You are thirsty. All around you the land is hot and thirsty as well. The trees creak from stiffness and the grass crackles as you step on it. Everything looks worn and tired. You feel very tired as well. The barn is falling apart. The windmill is rusted and is barely able to spin.

You walk over to the well which is located in the center of the yard. You lower a bucket into the well and pull it back up, but the bucket is empty. The well appears to be dry. You look down into the depths of the well and see nothing at first. Then after a few moments you notice a touch of light. Something has reflected the sky from above you. Water!

You descend into the well to investigate. There are stones for you to grab onto. There is enough room in the well for you to move. It is not cramped. You aren't afraid. As you descend, you look up to see the circle of light from the top of the well grow smaller and smaller. You continue descending several more feet. It is growing cooler. You reach the bottom of the well. The ground is dry and hard—except for one area that seems moist.

You kneel down and begin to dig. You dig into the earth with your hands. As you feel more moistness, you dig faster until your hands push into a pool of water. You cup some water in your hands and drink. As you drink, the water begins to rise. You float on the water as it quickly starts to fill the well. You are buoyed up and up as the water pushes its way to the surface of the well. The circle of light grows larger. You reach the top of the well but the water continues over the edge.

You are now standing on the grass watching as the water begins to quench the dry earth around you. It flows gently over the land—not as a flood, but as a life-giving essence. The water subsides quickly. You look into the well to see the water level close to the top. All around you, nature is responding to the water that you have released from within the well. Take a moment to see the trees, bushes, birds, and small animals drink in the water and gain strength. The trees sway gently in the wind and your house welcomes you as you enter it.

Everything is refreshed and invigorated. The water from the well has brought life again. You have dug down deep within yourself and found a source of strength that is never-ending. You feel a renewed sense of optimism and enthusiasm to continue with even the smallest chore.

Take a few moments to absorb this scene. Let it refresh and enliven you with the knowledge that there is a well of Spirit inside you at this very moment. You can tap into it at anytime by focusing on the inner source and digging beneath the surface images. After a while open your eyes and look around. Bring your newly sparked enthusiasm into your world today.

A Prayer on Commitment

Dear Gabriel,

Stand with me as I uncover the well of commitment from within my soul self. Please assist me to access the wisdom of the higher self so that I may understand the divine plan of the Creator. Help me to see day-by-day the value in the path I have chosen. I dedicate my heart and mind to the divine will as it is made apparent through the integration of the self.

This I ask of you through the universal Christ energy, Amen.

*Let it refresh and enliven you with the knowledge
that there is a well of Spirit inside you at this very moment.*

20

Creating Change:
An Exercise with Gabriel

ENERGY IS CONSTANTLY swirling around us. We are moved by energy in our work place, in the place we live, in the nation we are a part of. Cycles come and go, and we move along with their impulses. The seasons bring their own changes. Energies of the day and of the night move within our space and we respond to them. All life consists of energy. And here you are: in the center of your world, with the power to choose and the power to act.

Creating change means making choices to move the energy of our own being out into the world for experience. We may be reluctant to change (use our energy for new experiences) because we have experienced sorrow or pain of some kind linked to changes in the past. If we desire something, consider that there is something to learn about ourselves within that desire. Our desires culminate in experiences. We use our thoughts, words, and actions to move the energy we have access to in order to manifest forms and modify substances. It is in this process that we learn. Those who fear change are afraid to learn—afraid of their own desires. Yet soul extended itself into the world to learn—it desired to learn!

Gabriel urges you to find the strength to create change in your life by following your desires. He comes to help you act and accomplish within this world. The four Archangels are cornerstones of a foundation upon which you can build. Each of them is important.

You cannot easily create change without viewing your motivations and seeing truth. Michael assists you to see the truth of your motivations. To create change without seeing truth can bring you heartache.

If you do not connect with your emotional self, then the creations you manifest may be skewed by incomplete perceptions. Raphael can help you connect to your emotions. Viewing your motivations truthfully while feeling and then expressing your emotions enables you to properly decide which actions (acts of accomplishment) you wish to manifest in your life.

What do you wish to be remembered for? How would you like to be viewed by your loved ones after you have left this earth? What will be your contribution to humanity during this lifetime on earth? It is not only manifestation of forms and substances that are accomplishments. Being is an act of accomplishment as well—so too is acceptance and integration. The integration of your self-segments is one of the most important tasks that you can accomplish.

Energy is the substance we use to form our experience. Some acts require a greater expenditure of energy to accomplish than others. One particular act is not greater than another. Energy is one. It moves in harmony with the Creator.

The choice to create is up to us. The Creating Change exercise has two parts. Part one will help you define what you need and wish to accomplish. Part two will help you define the steps to create the change you have decided upon.

Using the Change Summary Expansion Sheet

The first step of this exercise is to determine what you need and wish to create in your life. This could be something new, such as learning a new skill or craft. You could also wish to create better relationships with your loved ones. In the latter case, you are changing a situation that already exists. Your need or wish could even be as simple as writing a letter to your sibling, or just taking a walk!

In order to help you to focus on the steps required to change, we've included the *Change Summary Expansion* sheet. We've filled out one and included it in this chapter as a sample. There is also a blank *Change Summary Expansion* sheet in Appendix B that you can make copies of for your personal use.

The purpose of the summary sheet is to focus on tasks that you wish to accomplish. Remember, where you place your attention, you place your energy. As you place energy, you transfer it from one locale to another. This, in and of itself, creates change by causing other forms and substances around you to move in reaction.

Place the summary sheet in front of you. Close your eyes. Now allow yourself to view your feelings. What are some of the things that you have been "just putting off" until later? These things may be difficult tasks in themselves or they may be things that require you to change. Change is hard, it is scary—but it is life. Change, growth, death, and birth are each part of the endless cycles of life.

Open your eyes and write down at least three, and up to five, things that you have been putting off, but know that you should do. Use one line on the summary sheet for each task. Do not fill in the "Need Level" or "Completed" columns at this time.

Now close your eyes again. Allow yourself to view your desires. What are some things that would make you very happy? Think of what you have longed for, but have given up hope of ever achieving. This can be as simple as taking a hot bubble bath every day, or as complex as writing a novel. Take a few moments for this, but don't linger too long. We'll look at each in greater detail later.

Open your eyes and write down at least three, and up to five, wishes or desires that you have dreamed of, but haven't yet brought into manifestation. Once again, use only one line on the summary sheet for each of the wishes or desires. Do not fill in the "Need Level" or "Completed" columns on the sheet at this time.

After completing the first two steps, take a moment to review all of the tasks you have written down. Your next step is to assign a numeric value—with 1 being the most important to 10 being the least important—to each of the tasks. Each entry should have a different value. Go through the form and assign the numeric value of your choice to each task in the "Need Level" column. Take a short time to do this step.

Refer to the sample *Change Summary Expansion* sheet on page 146. On it you can see four tasks we knew we needed to do, but had been putting off until another time. We have also written down four wishes or desires and assigned to each of the tasks on the sheet a need level from 1 through 10.

Continue with the exercise by first determining if multiple steps are needed in order to complete the task. If multiple steps are needed for a task, you can use the *Change Detail Expansion* sheet to help you with defining and completing those steps.

Using the Change Detail Expansion Sheet

If the task you have written down on the *Change Summary Expansion* sheet requires multiple steps to accomplish, you may find the detail sheet very helpful. A sample is included after this explanation. There is also a blank sheet in appendix B, which you can copy for your personal use. Here are the steps to using the *Change Detail Expansion* sheet.

Step 1. Review the task summary line. Close your eyes and relax. Visualize the situation or desire in the form of the experience that currently exists. Take a moment and allow not only visual images to come to you, but also the feeling of what it would be like to accomplish the task. Now see and feel yourself taking concrete steps to completing the task. Interact with the personalities and parts of yourself that you would need to when physically completing the task in the outer world.

Step 2. Open your eyes and describe, under the heading "Describe Accomplishing the Task," your vision of manifestation and completion. Use more paper if you need to. This is not a step-by-step description, but reflects the feelings and images as if the task were completed.

Step 3. Now write down a positive affirmation that you can repeat to yourself regarding the task. You can use this affirmation daily. Phrase the affirmation in a way that respects all the self-segments and honors yourself. Be loving and gentle.

Step 4. Turn the *Change Detail Expansion* sheet to the reverse side, where there are several lines for you to fill in. Use as many lines as you need here. On each line, fill in a specific sub-task that must be performed in order to complete the overall task. Do not fill in the "Order" and "Completed" columns at this time.

Step 5. Go through all the sub-tasks that you have written down and assign them a logical completion order. Assign the number 1 for the first sub-tasks incrementing the number for each of the subsequent sub-tasks. Do this until each sub-task has a number in the "Order" column.

Creating Change

An Exercise with Gabriel

Change Summary Expansion Sheet

Date: 2-4-98   Time: 7:00 p.m.

	Task To Accomplish	Need Level	Completed
1.	Write a letter to my cousin	5	
2.	Write a letter to my aunt	6	
3.	Start saving a small amount of money weekly	4	
4.	Drink less diet soda & more herbal teas	2	
5.	Do an open stage comedy act	8	
6.	Clean and organize home & personal papers	7	
7.	Focus on integrating & accepting my mother's death	1	
8.	Fix the leaking faucets in the washroom	3	
9.			
10.			

Creating Change
Steps to Change Detail Sheet: Side A

Date: 2-4-98   Time: 7:15 p.m.

Task To Accomplish: *Focus on integrating & accepting my mother's death*

Describe accomplishing the task

This task is to begin a conscious focus on the experience of my mother's death when I was a teenager. I see myself accepting this experience and healing my pain. This will allow me to gain a greater understanding of my life as well as honor my mother and myself.

Your Positive Affirmation of Accomplishment

I ask the help of the Archangels as I begin to focus on this issue. With the lessons of awareness I have already incorporated into my life I will bravely and honestly face all issues related to my mother's death.

Creating Change
Steps to Change Detail Sheet: Side B

Step	Order	Completed
* Browse book stores or libraries for books on dying.	2	
* Consciously think of a memory of my mother every day.	1	
* Write letters to my brother & aunts to talk about my mother's life.	6	
* Try the "Charting Your Life" exercise on this issue.	3	
* Write a letter to my deceased mother.	4	
* Talk with my son and daughter about their grandmother.	5	
* Talk with other people whose mother also died when they were young.	7	

Completing the Exercise

You should now have one *Change Summary Expansion* sheet and up to ten *Change Detail Expansion* sheets filled out and in front of you. Each day, starting with today, you should review the summary sheet and follow these steps:

Step 1. Find the lowest numbered item that is still not completed. If you wrote a *Change Detail Expansion* sheet for the task, then consult the detail sheet as outlined in step two, below, otherwise simply do the task that you are looking at. Do it the day you are reviewing it, if at all possible. Tasks that do not have multiple steps should require only a single action to accomplish. When you have completed the task, mark an "X" in the "Completed" column on the *Change Summary Expansion* sheet. Do not move on to the next task until you have taken some steps toward the current task! If you complete the task in question, start at the beginning of this step with the next goal. If you have completed all tasks on your list, then the whole exercise is finished.

Step 2. To complete this step, you should have already filled out a *Change Detail Expansion* sheet. Review the back of the sheet, where you have written down all the sub-tasks that must be accomplished to complete the main task. Choose the next sub-task that has not been completed and perform it. Perform as many sub-tasks as you can at this time. Always perform as least one sub-task each day. As you complete the sub-task, place an "X" in the "Completed" column and move to the next sub-task. When you have completed all sub-tasks, go back to the *Change Summary Expansion* sheet, mark an "X" in the "Completed" column and return to step one of this exercise. Do as many steps as comfortable in your day, but do at least one task or sub-task each day!

This expansion exercise is inspired by the Archangel Gabriel. It will help you move energy in specific patterns to achieve the experience you desire. It will help you carry out your responsibilities at times when you find it hard to motivate yourself. As energy begins to move, based on your actions, further changes will become easier to initiate. There is great joy and excitement in change. Creation can be (and is) fun in many ways.

As you create change by moving energy with your thoughts, words, and actions remember each Archangel's purpose, process, and power. Look to the lessons you have learned under their loving guidance. If you operate from the integrated self, what you manifest will not only benefit yourself but all those around you.

Energy is the substance we use
to form our experience.

Section 5

The Archangel Uriel

And in those days the angel Uriel
answered and said to me:
"Behold, I have shown thee everything, Enoch, and I have
revealed everything to thee that thou shouldst see
this sun and this moon,
and the leaders of the stars of the heaven
and all those who turn them,
their tasks and times and departures."

—Enoch III:80

21

Uriel: The Archangel of Love and Beauty

THE LAST OF the four Archangels is Saint Uriel. One of the least depicted and painted Archangels, the most common image is that of Uriel standing with a small flame burning in the palm of his hand. Uriel has also been spoken of as a prophet and has been painted carrying a scroll of sorts or a book in his hand. The knowledge of the prophet represents the soul self sending its impulses down through the higher self to the conscious self.

As Michael has helped you to increase your power of seeing, Raphael your power of feeling, and Gabriel your power of acting, Uriel comes to you to help you to increase your power of being. It is through the power to be that we come to appreciate. Through the process of appreciation we bring more love, beauty, and awareness into our lives.

The Experience of Being

The experience of being is to be at rest but also to be active. It appears to be passive, yet it is an experience that is fully involved and moving with the energy of the Creator. It is as glorious and significant an experience in the ebb as well as in the flow cycles of life. Defying classification, the experience of being is beyond the concept of soul-infusion. It is beyond the concept of concepts themselves.

The power to be is increased by relaxing. Paradoxically, this relaxing leads us to a state of awareness that contains the knowledge of life, its purpose, and our position in the universe and all the worlds of creation. It is through relaxing into the present moment that we become aware of the allness of life. We find that we are in, and have always been in, the flow of the divine life force: the Holy Spirit.

PETER'S STORY

An Experience of "Being"

The weekend after I had first met Linda, I went to a spiritual retreat that she had been planning to attend. After the day's lessons and events, Linda and I decided to take a walk around the beautiful grounds of the retreat center, which was nestled in a wooded area of east-central Minnesota. It was early September and the weather was warm; the sky was clear without a cloud.

It was evening and the beauty of God's creation was as evident then as it must have been since the dawn of time. The black sky was dotted with stars that seemed to be suspended in the heavens. I felt as if I could reach out and touch both the moon and stars right up there in the night sky. As I walked with Linda, a strange and comforting sense of peace washed all over me. We sat on a bench and held hands. We began to talk.

The perfection of the moment was exquisite. Each word spoken was as if it were a piece of a puzzle that fit perfectly on the first attempt to piece it together. There was no strain of thought nor action. No pain of any kind existed in this state. All energy centers were calm and flowing in a peaceful fashion. As Linda and I spoke, I realized that the words that came from me flowed easily. They came from a central core of my being so effortlessly that I was amazed, in one sense, at their wisdom. Yet on the other hand the flowing of the moment seemed completely natural.

All of nature around us seemed to comply with this experience of being. The stars hung high in the night sky as if they were portals to Heaven shining their love upon us. And the moon reflected the sun, signifying that God's love is ever-burning for us, even though we may have been in the darkness of the night.

Time seemed to stop in this experience. There was no yesterday, nor was there a tomorrow. All was contained in the moment and yet the moment was not stuffed nor cluttered. Each piece and part was in perfect alignment with all others. This mysterious and wonderful state was healing both of us, although we were conscious of already being whole. It was a gift of God.

How can we hope to know all things with our mind alone? How can we hope to experience the fullness of life with just our feelings or our bodies? This experience of "being" encompassed, but did not confine, all of these areas and more. All energy centers were showered in complete and absolute love.

I shall never forget this experience of being and I shall strive to "be" with the assistance of the Archangels and the guidance of Uriel. I believe that this state of being is the ultimate state of healing that the Archangels Plan of Healing for Mankind will lead each of us to. For in it is the completeness of all the energies of the universe, our souls, the Angels, Archangels, and God.

Love: Beyond the Senses

Do you recall the chart on the energy centers (chakras) from chapter 4? These energy centers are constantly spinning, processing energy in and out of the body system. Similar to our physical breathing, this process is automatic. As an individual comes in contact with another individual, a relationship is formed. The relationship creates a line between the energy centers of the two beings. These lines can be considered as cords between the two individuals.

The cords that develop between beings in a relationship are real entities. While not separate beings, the cords are actual connections made from psychic/etheric matter. They start small at the chakra centers and bond one to the other. Energy is given and received through the cords.

If an excess of energy is sent though a cord that has not yet developed the proper strength to handle the flow, burn-out of the wire can occur and then the cord may even break. Therefore, build the cord into a larger conduit of energy before sending an overpowering current through it. Overpowering the growing cord can break it.

The same is true of asking for too much energy from a cord that hasn't yet fully developed. Cords between two individuals can develop on one or a combination of the energy centers. A well-balanced relationship usually has more than one energy center with bonds or cord connections.

EXERCISE

On Connecting

Go into a relaxed meditative state and visualize the person with whom you are having a relationship (or are entering a relationship, or leaving a relationship).

After a few moments, begin to sense where the energy is in your body. Keep thinking of the other individual. The first area of awareness is probably the most active cord area at the present moment.

Examine it briefly. What is its size? What is its state of health? Is it strong or weak? What energy center is it attached to?

If you wish to restore the cord to good health, you can try the following. Remember, this is your choice. Each of us have the freedom to choose in a relationship. Just as you extend your hand, another may extend or refuse.

To restore the cord, try sending loving vibrations through it—but only to the magnitude of its acceptance. Don't forget that the cord is attached at the other end! Should you send too much energy down or through the cord and the other person cannot accept it, what do you think happens to that energy? Prior approval is a good way to increase the energy flow.

This information is not meant to influence you away from sending love to those you cherish. It is more a realization for those who wish to understand the psychic/esoteric method and how overdoing it can break the cord that has been formed into a reality.

To increase cord size and capability, be honest, truthful, and secure in your own being. Allow physical time for this building process to occur. For some it is also a matter of breaking old ties (cords) so that there is space for the newer relationship cords. Timing and method are dependent on the individuals involved.

Let divine love guide and nourish you. Let beautiful thoughts emanate from you. Love yourself and allow others to be who they are.

Beauty is in the Eye of the Beholder

Love is the essence of life. Loving ourselves is the first step to loving others. If we treat ourselves poorly, how can we truly love others? The way we treat ourselves affects all others around us.

If you have gained an understanding of the effect of moving energy, then you realize that ALL actions affect the moving of energy. One action affects another, which in turn affects another, and so on. So it behooves us to begin the process of love by knowing ourselves. We come to know ourselves by self-examination. This self-examination must be accompanied with acceptance and without self-condemnation.

As you choose to love yourself by your actions and your thoughts, you come to appreciate the beauty of life. This appreciation is the natural result of practicing the art of being. We can increase our appreciation of life by practicing the 365 Days of Learning and Appreciation exercise inspired by Uriel. It can help you to open your heart and give value to those aspects which you have forgotten to give thanks for or that you didn't know existed.

It has been said that the outer world is a reflection of the inner world. The following short exercise is designed to help you see the beauty of yourself. It is not an easy exercise. It requires that you apply all that you have learned with Saint Michael, Raphael, and Gabriel. Appreciating your own inner and outer beauty is important and helps you to appreciate the beauty in the world. A healthy self-love is important for living a balanced, loving life.

Look into the Mirror

Pick a time when you can spend ten to fifteen minutes alone without interruption. For this exercise you will need a mirror. It is suggested that you stand alone in front of your bathroom mirror. Have a small pad of paper with you and a pen or a pencil.

E X E R C I S E

On Beauty

The first step is to look into the mirror and simply view yourself. Look at your hair, your eyes, your face. As you view those parts of yourself, take note about your thought processes. What is your inner self telling you? Can you use the power of seeing to uncover any hidden criticisms that a part of you holds against yourself? Write down any feelings which are critical of yourself.

Now with the feeling power of Raphael, try to express to yourself the emotions that these criticisms cause within you. Identify the emotion as you have been taught, then move to the root emotion for complete expression.

Next, for each statement of criticism that you wrote, write a statement that accepts the fear of the loss of love. Take and expand that statement into a positive affirmation that empowers you rather than limits you.

Now look at your list of affirmations and say each one in succession as you look into the mirror at yourself. When you are done take another few moments to close your eyes and relax. Breathe in and out slowly. Do this for a minute while relaxing.

Now, open your eyes and look into the mirror to see the beauty within you. Accept yourself as you are and allow yourself to give and to receive love.

During your study under the Archangel Uriel, practice seeing beauty in yourself. Take time in your day to appreciate hidden things, as well as those things that are easily apparent to you in your world. Remember to live in the moment and allow yourself to just be, whether you are at work or at home.

Continue to process your experiences. This will help you to keep your heart open. Give the love that you wish to give, and receive the love of others who wish to give to you as they can—each in their own way. Do not forget the love of life itself as it manifests through the Holy Spirit into the worlds of form and substance.

The love of Spirit is not meant to be a replacement for human love nor the experience of human embodiment, for the human need is a spiritual need. We believe we have chosen to be on earth to learn. If this is true, then we honor and respect life by participating with courage and joy and by taking the chance to open our hearts to our fellow beings. The opportunities are many and the rewards are great, for love is the most precious attribute that the Creator has given us. Let us love and be loved, now and forevermore.

Through the process of appreciation we bring
more love, beauty, and awareness into our lives.

22

Love, A Choice You Make:
The Powers, Purpose, and Process of Uriel

THE MAIN PURPOSE of the energy emanating from the Archangel Uriel is to assist with the flowering of the Godly attributes of love, beauty, and awareness within each of us. This is symbolized by the eternal flame in the palm of Uriel's hand, which signifies the undying love of the Creator. It illuminates the world so that we may see the beauty in it and in ourselves. Finally, the flame gives warmth, symbolizing the awareness of the heart aflame with the love of God.

The main power of the energy stream emanating from Uriel is that of love. God so loved the world to send into it the light, as signified by the flame, for us to see the way. The greatest of all the attributes of God is love.

Through following the guidance of the four Archangels you have attained a deeper insight into yourself and into life. As you dedicate yourself to a life of honesty, healing, and commitment so shall you find that a flame of love burns within you, and it burns forever more.

The flame of love inside you is now uncovered for the world to see and for you to experience unfettered by destructive tendencies and habits. The infusion of the divine energies of the Archangels is completed as the Archangel Uriel bestows upon you the full awareness of love and beauty.

Increasing your Appreciation

How can we create an attitude of gratitude, appreciation, and thankfulness in our lives? How can we increase our heart's awareness of all that is good in our lives? The answer is the same—to consciously focus each and every day on the blessings in your life. The following prayer is an example of how to consciously focus on the present moment and thus give value to that which we appreciate:

I am so thankful, God, that you have given me ears to listen, eyes to see, and a heart with which to love. Thank you for all the people in my life who are as mirrors to me, teaching me who I am and how to love myself and others.

As a soul having a human experience, we look for opportunities to share our awareness of soul's consciousness with the world. We can help increase the world's awareness of the availability of the divine energy of God's love by focusing on our blessings and by unwrapping the gift that we are and giving it to ourselves and to the world.

Why is an attitude of gratitude so important in our lives? Because it creates a consciousness of love and appreciation within us. No longer are we focusing on what is hard or wrong with our lives, rather we are focusing on the present and on all that is already wonderful in our lives. By creating and staying awake within this awareness, we create a receptive consciousness into which more blessings can flow.

LINDA'S STORY

Gratitude and Appreciation

If your mate actually said something like the following to you, each and every day, how would it make you feel? "Dearest Peter, I love you so much and I appreciate all that you do every day." They are simple words and it doesn't take a long time to say them, but they go a long way in making me realize how much I do love him and appreciate all aspects of him each day. The words probably make Peter feel good, too! But most important is what the words do for me. They remind me not to take him or his wonderful being for granted. They remind me of how blessed I am to be in a loving and growing relationship. They remind me of who I am, of how blessed I am, and of how much I have to give back to him, and to the world.

These words aren't only for those in marital relationships. They are for us to say to our children, our friends, our family members, and even our pets. They are words to love and grow and live by. We need to say them to our loved ones not just for their sake, but for our own sake. These words will help to keep our love alive, our hearts open, and our minds creatively present.

When you call upon the Archangel Uriel, you will feel a warm, sweet, and compassionate presence. You will also feel a sense of lightness and humor, for he is very gifted in revealing to us his funny side. I feel his presence around and within me whenever I am working on cultivating this attitude of thankfulness.

We work on this gratitude aspect by being prayerful upon waking in the morning; while we say grace at mealtimes; and again at bedtime as we say thanks for a day full of life and blessings. There are so many things to be grateful for!

Living in Minnesota, as Peter and I do, we are especially thankful for the bright rays of the sun, warming our bodies and lighting the dark, cold winter days. As each day presents itself to us we can find more and more things to be grateful for as we come to live in a state of appreciation. As we mentioned above, appreciation brings us into the moment, and as we all know, that is where we truly live and have our being.

Love Me Tender

Learning to say tender words of love and appreciation to others is hard if we haven't been taught how. It helps to say these words first to yourself, and then to your loved ones. Sometimes it is easier to write a love note to someone, rather than saying the words right away. You can ease into an attitude of appreciation by doing this.

It is hard to say loving and appreciative words to someone, even to God, if you aren't feeling like you are being loved and appreciated yourself. That is why it is so important to first say words of appreciation to yourself, about yourself. It is part of the re-parenting to be discussed later in the chapters on dreams and the emotions.

The more you are able to speak and write these loving words, the more they will be reciprocated by your loved ones in a way that is most comfortable for them. We can teach them and ourselves what we need to hear, for they may not guess our heart's desire unless we communicate it to them. We may not know exactly what we need to hear until we bring it into physical manifestation by speaking or writing the words.

You Are Not Alone

Sometimes our hearts become bitter and hardened by painful traumas such as divorce and custody battles; loss of a valued job; loss of a loved one or a disabling disease or accident. We may feel like we have no hope or that God and the world itself are against us. We feel completely alone, ripped apart and numb. Sometimes a cold wall of bitterness forms around our hearts to seemingly protect our vulnerability.

In this time of pain and darkness it is hard to feel thankful for anything, and it is difficult to reach out for help because of the fear it will make us vulnerable again. We are afraid to love, afraid to give, and we hide behind a wall of hardness and pain. We say to those of you suffering in such a manner—you are not as alone as it appears. There are people and beings in your life who care deeply about you right now. They may be afraid to show you how much they care because they don't feel they should intrude on your grief or they don't feel they have the right words that will lift your heart. Please allow yourself to reach out to these people and let them know you need help.

It is not a sign of weakness to reach out for help, it is a sign of strength and self-knowledge. If you have isolated yourself and don't have many people with whom you interact daily, reach out to old friends, people you haven't seen for years, even if it has been ten or twenty years or more. These people still care about you and hold you in their hearts.

Linda and Peter have friends whom they haven't seen for over twenty years and they still think of them often with love and fondness and cherishing in their hearts. The love and support of these friends, if you let them know you need them, can lead you back to the warmth and love and caring that is the nature of your heart and soul.

Linda went through a very difficult divorce about ten years ago. During that process she found herself in the very situation depicted above. In desperation, she reached out to old friends whom she hadn't seen for years—to her surprise and joy they reached back and supported her with loving arms and helped her to see the light and love within herself and others again.

The healing process took time, but with their help she was able to trust again. Her friends responded from the abundance of love within themselves and from the wisdom gained from their own past experiences of trauma and healing. Let your friends help you, let the kindness of strangers and family help you—don't be afraid to reach out! Listen to their healing words—they may not always say the right thing, but what they do say is meant with the best of intentions and care. You do not have to follow their advice, simply thank them for it and for listening, and ask them to please continue trying to support you, even if you cannot respond well because of your hurt, anger, or depression.

This is a good time to pray and call upon the Angels, Archangels (particularly Uriel and Raphael), and God as well. Praying helps to reconnect you with the love and wisdom that is buried in your heart, and while our prayers are not always answered exactly in the way we may expect, they are answered lovingly and abundantly; for love is the very substance of the universe and it calls to each of us, the children of God.

The Angels are constantly sending vibrations of love and healing to us, and if our hearts are closed because of too much pain, they often inspire friends and family—sometimes even strangers—to give of themselves out of their own hearts, which are filled with love and abundance. So, if you are in pain, reach out. If you see anyone else in pain, reach out with love, acceptance, and the abundance that you presently enjoy.

Strive not to judge or advise (this might take a little work), but rather listen. Be available for an old friend or person in need. Stretch out your hand to them. Make time for them in your busy life, for there is great joy in giving, and you will create space for many blessings to flow both to you and to the one in need.

We are dedicating our lives to extending the Archangels' messages of healing to the world. Let us each help one another, let us each be a blessing to one another, and may we all find an abundance of gratitude, blessings, and love in our lives. We are sharing what we have learned from our own painful experiences and also what we have learned from love and joy, and from our awareness of the presence and care of the Angels and the Archangels.

Linda never expected to heal from her trauma, yet she did. She never expected to be the recipient of the love and care her friends showered upon her, yet, because she reached out, she did! She had fully resigned herself to living a life alone, without a partner. Yet the grace of God is limitless, and at the proper time and in a totally unexpected place, Peter arrived in her life, complete with all his gifts of creativity, love, grace—and with a set of his own problems.

Rarely can we, as a soul having a human experience, say that we have no problems to attend to. Problems are to be seen as opportunities to learn and grow. The love and support of friends, family, and the beings of Heavenly worlds help us to sustain our emotional, mental, and physical balance during these challenging times. Just as a stone becomes more beautiful as it is broken and polished by the rough waves of the ocean, so too do we uncover the beauty within as life polishes us and the divinity of our inner spiritual nature is revealed. May we learn to view our challenges as opportunities for growth and change, and continue to be able to love and give to others during difficult, as well as abundant times, in our lives. Let us never lose sight of the love that is within us and within others.

A List Of Blessings: Cultivating an Attitude of Appreciation, Gratitude, and Thankfulness

On this note, Linda would now like to share with you a list of blessings she keeps posted on the refrigerator as a daily reminder of all that is good and loving in her life. Daily she asks herself the questions: "What are my blessings today?" "What challenges are presenting themselves?" "How can I learn from these challenges?" "In what way can I reach out and help others today?"

You may want to create your own list of blessings to help you live in an attitude of thanksgiving and abundance. You may also want to formulate some questions to ask yourself daily to promote self-growth and to create ways to extend your love and gifts to the world. The Archangel Uriel is sending vibrations of love, beauty, and appreciation to help you and the world, right now. Choose to open to the care and love of this beautiful vibrational energy. Doing so will strengthen these characteristics in you and through you to the world.

Linda's List of Blessings

1. Dear Lord, thank you for the blessing of my physical body. Thank you for my legs, which take me where I need to go; for my hands, whose touch can warm and heal; for my voice, with which I can communicate; for my fingers, with which I can type and extend messages of learning and growth. For there are many in hospitals or at home, struggling with pain and disabilities.

2. Dear Lord, thank you for the home that shelters me and my loved ones from the cold but beautiful Minnesota winters. There are many in the world who are homeless.

3. Dear Lord, thank you for the love and acceptance of my friends and family—they who have carried me in the dark times with the gift of themselves. There are many people in the world right now who feel afraid, alone, and friendless.

4. Dear Lord, thank you for the gift of my loving husband Peter, who is as a mirror to me, always teaching and inspiring me as he generously shares his warmth, learning, creativity, curiosity, and strength. For there are many single, divorced, or widowed who walk the path alone, without a partner to encourage or sustain them.

5. Dear Lord, thank you for Peter's intelligence and his commitment to hard work—for it provides us with the necessities of life and it frees me to concentrate on building a home within which your presence is welcomed and your messages can be transcribed and communicated to the world.

6. Dear Lord, thank you for the gift that our children are, for although they challenge us as only teenagers and young adults can, there are many who are childless.

7. Dear Lord, thank you for the gift of my father, for although he is now getting elderly and more frail; there are many in the world who are fatherless.

8. Dear Lord, thank you for the gift of being born in the U.S.A., a land of peace and democracy, for there are many born in countries torn by war, famine, and lack of opportunity.

What is your list of blessings? Try this short exercise. You may find your heart opening like a flower to the sun.

The Wisdom of the Archangels

We thank all the Archangels for sharing the blessings of God on our journey. Michael has shown us our power of seeing so that we may understand who we are today. Raphael has shown us our power of feeling so that we may heal the wounds of the past and express ourselves today so that we may remain open to the spirit of life. Gabriel has shown us our power of acting so that we may pursue and accomplish our life's mission.

And finally Uriel, one of the most mysterious and little-known Archangels, has shown us our power of being so that we may come to appreciate the love, beauty, and awareness of life itself. A state of soul-infusion is reached.

The wisdom that you have cultivated from working with the Archangels will continue to benefit you throughout your life. And while we are on earth to experience, learn, and accomplish; always remember that we are *beings*. Uriel has helped us learn how to appreciate life by just being.

It is not a sign of weakness to reach out for help,
it is a sign of strength and self-knowledge.

23

A Message from Uriel

Heaven is Inside You Right Now!

Live each moment as if it were your last. Cull each experience for each layer of reality it presents to you. Continue to speak your truth in each relationship; the whole, complete, loving truth. Truth is loving—it is the only love you have. Be not afraid to reveal your whole heart. As you speak, so shall you grow, and so shall your relationships deepen.

Be gentle but continue your diligent search for truth and beauty in all experiences. Fear not to clarify the truth—truth expands, fear contracts. Let the outer storm reflect the inner storm, burning away doubt and inner conflict so that the simple, honest lightness of your full being is free to expand in ways undreamed of and thus far unimagined.

Appreciate deeply and reflect on the absolute truth and beauty of yourself. At the same time appreciate the divergent inner perceptions and reality of your fellow man. For each perception is a layer of your ultimate reality. It can only enrich you to consider each other's point of view. Do not be concerned if it does not resonate within your personal truth. It is simply another layer of truth. There are many paths to the truth. It is each of our jobs to let our light shine onto our own path while respecting the heart, beliefs and beauty of every path no matter how narrow or rigid it might appear to us.

Honor the truth of each perspective because it is verily one of the layers of truth. As we peel away the layers of truth so shall we reveal God's ultimate truth. Your individual truths should simply seek to establish a thread of commonality. The absolute beauty is in their differences—both on a microcosmic level and on the deeper outer levels manifested as our world or universal soul. Layers upon layers, dreams within dreams. Connect your inner dreams to physical matter.

Heaven is inside you now because the grace of God is in you now. Within you is the memory and vibrational imprint of the experience of being in the heavenly worlds of the Creator. By focusing your attention on that which you are—you increase your awareness of that which is.

Appreciation brings contentment and contentment fosters honesty. If you are feeling discontented, identify what it is you are feeling and move to change your circumstances, attitude, or understanding about the situation. Find in it the kernel of the Creator. Learn to appreciate the purpose of your discontent. For nothing is without meaning in your world.

The great poets strive to describe the wonders of life with their pen and the written word. As they have imbued themselves into the life stream, so too can you feel and experience those states of divine wonder and humanity.

Appreciation is an acceptance of the divine Creator's plan. You can appreciate the lessons that you learn from living in your world. Learn to appreciate change, for it is through change that we experience the different parts of creation, and it is through change that you manifest your experiences in your world. It is through change that pain becomes pleasure and pleasure becomes pain. It is through change and transmutation that you learn and grow within the worlds that the soul has chosen to extend itself into.

You have worked diligently on yourself through the tutoring of the Archangel Michael who has helped you to remove the scales from your eyes so that you may honestly see the truth of your motivations; the Archangel Raphael who has shown you that you must heal your heart by expressing your feelings of unresolved pain so that you can live attuned to the life force in loving alignment; and the Archangel Gabriel who has come to you and continues to be with you showing you how to bring into manifestation your life's mission. He shows you the way to your own strength.

As those three Archangels help you, so too will I. My hand is outstretched with the flame of knowledge and awareness. This flame burns forever more. It is the flame of divine light and love. It warms the heart as you move about in the world.

Do you remember when you were a little child looking at the sky, sun, moon, and the stars? The wonder of life was fresh and new to you. That wonder exists now. The world has not essentially changed. Remove the insulation around yourself with the help of the four Archangels so that you may at once experience the world in its totality. You leave yourself vulnerable when the heart is uncovered—but how can you lock your heart away in a safe and hope to live a life of love and fullness?

To appreciate means to give value to. As you move through your day, silently give thanks for the functions of your heart, mind, and soul. Give thanks for the air that you breathe and the bed that you sleep in at night. Give thanks for your loved ones and those who you have disagreements with. Give thanks for the tools that you use to create, sustain, and nourish yourselves. Give thanks and realize that much has been given to you.

I will be with you when called upon to guide you and assist you. I will teach you and help point you to the way of love, beauty, appreciation, and awareness. For I love and appreciate you as I do all life.

You may ask how can you appreciate your balding head, or your bulging midsection? I ask you how can you not appreciate these things? They are parts of the manifestation of your own life and of the life of the Creator. To not learn from your conditions is to close your eyes. It is to blindfold yourself.

The purpose, power, and process of myself is intertwined with the purpose, process, and powers of all the other Archangels. It is part of the divine plan of the Creator. It is in itself an endless spiral of growth, learning, and knowledge. This process is given in love for our eternal being.

I do not ask you to appreciate for the sake of appreciation. Feelings cannot be forced. You do yourself an injustice and are not living the truth if you do not honestly accept whatever it is you are feeling. The exercises that I give will help to focus you on the forms and substances of your world and kindle within you a remembrance of the attribute of appreciation.

Choosing to appreciate can help stimulate your feelings. In that kindling lies the truth. It is the beginning of the flame of appreciation that is the truth. Raphael can help you connect to your feelings again. He will help you heal any resistance you may feel toward appreciation by leading you to the fear of the loss of love that lies beneath this resistance.

Remember that you are in the world to experience. Take in the experience, process it, integrate it. That becomes your wisdom. Your projections become honest when they are honestly projected from the truth of what you are actually feeling. There is no reason to force nor fake your feelings. Seek the assistance of Raphael to heal your heart and to get in touch with who you really are.

Speak from the center of your being. That is your truth. It is the truth of your being. Speak from there and all will be well.

The meditations and exercises that I inspire are methods that help you focus on the aspects of love and appreciation. They are not ends unto themselves. Use them when you need assistance to focus on these divine attributes. As you water a plant to help its growth, so too does focusing your attention upon the divine attributes help them to grow in your life. And as the plant grows a small portion each day, invisible to the naked eye, so too does the love and appreciation of awareness and beauty grow within you daily. Until one day, in joy, you become aware of the flame within your heart.

When you do, imprint that memory upon your mind. Link that experience so that you can recall it when the winds of your world move your attention and focus. This will be your road map back to the flame of love.

I give this message to you in the universal Christ energy of the divine Creator.

*It is never too late to begin again, for a cycle
starting is a new experience in motion.*

24

Prayers and Meditations to Contact the Archangel Uriel

A Prayer on Love

Dear Uriel,

I pray to you to share with me your love and care so that I may be able to see the love that is within me and share it with the world, and with myself. Show me the way to the child within and guide me as I strive to accept the reality of my life as it is now.

This I ask of you through the universal Christ energy, Amen.

MEDITATION

On Uriel's Presence

Take a seat in an easy chair or lie on a bed. Loosen any tight fitting clothes. Use the method you are best suited to for relaxation (such as deep breathing). This will help you focus inwardly. Make sure that you will not be disturbed for 15 to 30 minutes. After your mind has quieted and your body is relaxed, continue with the rest of the meditation.

Imagine that you are alone on a journey. You are setting up camp for the evening. The sun is setting and you have found a place to bed down for the night. After setting up your sleeping area, you get ready to cook your dinner. You gather some wood for a small fire and place it in a circular pile on the dirt. The sky is now a dark blue and the stars are twinkling faintly. They are becoming brighter every minute.

You reach into your pocket for your matches but cannot find any. Searching through the rest of your gear you realize that your matches must have fallen out along the trail. You resign yourself to eating a cold dinner and covering up with extra blankets at bedtime. You start to open your food containers when you see a light coming from within the trees.

The light becomes brighter and you see a stranger emerge from the forest. He walks over to you. You are not afraid. He carries nothing with him, so you are confused about where the light is coming from. It seems to be coming from all around him in a soft glow. You realize that this is the Archangel Uriel.

He bends down next to the wood you have set up for the fire and opens the palm of his hand to reveal a flame of light. It does not burn, yet it is hot. You are amazed at the heat that is coming from such a small flame. The flame also warms your heart somehow. He places his hand on the sticks and they begin to catch fire. He withdraws his hand and the campfire begins to burn strongly.

You thank him for his help. As you look at him and into his eyes, you see a great love and beauty like you have never seen before. You see yourself reflected in his eyes. Speak to him if you wish, ask him any questions that you may have. Take a few minutes to be with Uriel.

After a while he bids farewell and walks away into the forest. You are alone again. You cook your food and begin to eat it. It warms your body. Everything is in a perfect state of balance. You feel an overwhelming love for all life. It pulses from within you in gentle waves of gratitude.

Continue in this state for as long as feels comfortable, and then slowly awaken yourself from the meditation. Open your eyes and look around. Feel the presence of Uriel as you go about your day reflecting on the love of simply living.

A Prayer on Beauty

Dear Uriel,

Please be with me as I learn to see the beauty in all creation. Help me to understand the beauty of all life's cycles; creation, maintenance, and dissolution. I strive to uncover the beauty of my own being for myself and the world to see and benefit from. May the beauty that is . . . impress upon me the beauty that has always been.

This I ask of you through the universal Christ energy, Amen.

MEDITATION

On Appreciation

Take a seat in an easy chair or lie on a bed. Loosen any tight fitting clothes. Use the method you are best suited to for relaxation (such as deep breathing). This will help you focus inwardly. Make sure that you will not be disturbed for 15 to 30 minutes. After your mind has quieted and your body is relaxed, continue with the rest of the meditation.

Imagine that you are seated next to a circular table in a circular room. There is a faint light spreading through the room like a mist.

The center of the table is well lit from above. There is nothing on the table. You notice that there are images on the walls of the room. They look like paintings in an art gallery. Each painting portrays a scene from your life.

There are scenes with your brothers or sisters, father or mother, son or daughter, and friends. You also see images of your possessions— your home, your car. To your surprise you see images of yourself as well—at work, at home, and at play.

Choose one image to focus on. As you focus upon it, the image suddenly appears as a three-dimensional hologram on the circular table in front of you. The image itself is dark, even though the table around it is bathed in a soft light.

Find something to appreciate in this image, whatever it may be, and however small it may be. As you begin to think of the value that the image represents to you, it begins to grow brighter. The more that you find value in it, the brighter and more full of life the image before you becomes, until the image is so life-like it startles you. A golden glow now surrounds the image. Meditate on the image and its contents for a few moments.

Next, focus on another picture from the wall of the room. It now appears on the table where the first image had been. This new image is also dark. As you did with the other image, find something that you value in it, however small. From there, try increasing the brightness of the image by finding value in it.

Work with as many images during this meditation as you wish. You need not work with them all. This room is always here. You may return to view the images and work with the circular hologram table again.

After you are done, open your eyes. Relax. As you move through the day, practice finding value (no matter how small) in the experiences of your day and the people you interact with. In this way you increase their value and your appreciation of them in your life. In appreciation you will find gratitude.

A Prayer on Appreciation

Dear Uriel,

I pray to you to be with me and to send me your energy as I review my life. I promise to you that I will look past the surface images. I will take the time to thank the Creator for the love and beauty in my life. I will strive to appreciate the presence of my loved ones and the Creator. Help me to cherish each moment of consciousness as a gift from God.

This I ask of you through the universal Christ energy, Amen.

By focusing your attention on that which you are—
you increase your awareness of that which is.

25

365 Days of Learning and Appreciation:
An Exercise with Uriel

EACH DAY OF life on this earth is precious. The sun rises, sharing its warmth with us. We move through our busy day attending to the duties we must perform in order to sustain our lives and the lives of those for whom we are responsible. Life does not stop for us. The world keeps turning, and we along with it, as if the earth itself were on a journey.

We have each had the experience of taking something in our life for granted and only when it was lost or left us did we realize the worth of that thing or person. Very often it is too late to retrieve what we have lost and we are left to move on with our life as the world spins on.

To appreciate something is to give it value. We appreciate something by finding the wonder within it and honoring it. We see the value in it and give thanks for it in our lives. This exercise, inspired by the Archangel Uriel, is entitled *365 Days of Learning and Appreciation.* It is designed to open your whole being to the love that is all around you.

From the food grown in the fields to the water that quenches our thirst, we give thanks for the nurturing and life-giving elements that we partake of each day. We also give thanks for the joy of the presence of our loved ones, our children, our partners, and our own consciousness. This exercise increases within us an appreciation for life in all its aspects!

On the following page are eighteen different topics with instructions. These eighteen topics and instructions are also included on cardstock in Appendix B. You can cut the cards out and use them for this exercise. There is an additional sheet of nine blank cards for you to create your own topics and instructions. Shuffle the cards and mix them. This is now your Deck of Appreciation.

Each of the cards gives you specific instructions. Follow the instructions as you are able. Some cards require physical situations that you may, for health or other reasons, be unable to follow. If this is the case, remove the card from the deck and choose another. Review all the cards. If in doubt about a certain card, remove it from your deck. Each card is described below. After reviewing the cards you will have a good idea of how to construct your nine optional cards.

Each time you do this exercise, shuffle the entire deck and pick one card. Follow the instructions as indicated and use the *Appreciation Experience Form* to record your reactions to the exercise. On the form are spaces for the date, day of the week, time, card number selected, and instructions on the card. A blank *Appreciation Experience Form* is included in Appendix B for your personal copying and use.

After following the instructions on the individual card and fulfilling its directives, you should fill out the two text boxes on the *Appreciation Experience Form*. One text box asks you to describe your experience in detail. If you need more room use the back of the form. The second text box asks you to write about what you have learned about appreciation by following the exercise as indicated on the chosen card. Take your time to think about your experience as you write.

By using this technique inspired by Archangel Uriel you will begin to rediscover the things and people in life that you have taken for granted. This technique can help you open your heart to the wonder of life that you once had as a child. It is that wonder that you had as you lay on the grass on a sunny day looking at the clouds and seeing the shapes and forms move across the sky. Try this technique daily. Create more cards for yourself as you come across new issues that you wish to explore with the loving presence and energy of Uriel.

The Angel Cards and their Instructions

1. **Eyes Closed:** For the period of one hour, blindfold your eyes. Use your hands to feel and your ears to hear. Do this in the middle of the day if possible. For safety, have a partner or helper nearby to avoid any accidents if you choose to move about.

2. **No Hands:** For the period of one hour, do not use your hands for any function at all. Do this in the middle of the day if possible.

3. **No Legs:** For the period of one hour, do not use your legs to walk. Do this in the middle of the day if possible. You may crawl or creep.

4. **No Talking:** For the period of twenty-four hours, do not use your voice to communicate in any way. You may use written communications.

5. **Hearing:** For the period of one hour, place cotton in your ears or wear ear plugs. This is to deaden sounds around you.

6. **Listening:** For the period of one-half hour, go out into nature and write down all the sounds that you hear. Relax.

7. **Vision:** Purchase a watercolor set and some paper. Go out into nature, pick a scene, and to the best of your ability duplicate its image on the paper.

8. **Fasting:** For the period of twenty-four hours, do not eat. Drink only water or fruit and vegetable juices. If unable to fast, give up one food item for the day (i.e., coffee or soft drinks).

9. **Separation:** For the period of one night, sleep separately from your spouse or relationship partner. If you are alone, sleep in a different room of your home. Write down your experience before seeing your partner again.

10. **Cleansing:** For the period of forty-eight hours, do not bathe or shower (this is best done on a weekend).

11. **Cleaning:** Wash one load of your laundry by hand in a wash tub or bath tub. Wring and hang dry.

12. **Electricity:** For the period of twenty-four hours, do not use any small appliances that use electricity or batteries (such as tv or radio).

13. **Shower:** Take one cold or cool shower.

14. **Writing:** Write a letter to a loved one. Imagine that loved one is no longer on this earth. Say all your heart would long to say.

15. **Reading:** Do not read anything intentionally for the period of 24 hours.

16. **Travel:** Do not ride in a car, bus, motor vehicle, or bicycle for the period of 24 hours.

17. **Alone:** Spend a day by yourself, from sunrise to sunset. Make sure to get up in time to see the sunrise and watch the sunset. Do not do any form of work or entertainment for this whole period. Be with yourself.

18. **Surprise:** Surprise a close friend, relative, or partner with something that you make. This could be food, a poem, or a gift of some other kind. Do not purchase this gift. You must make it.

On the following two pages are examples of this technique; one from Linda and one from Peter. We each chose an Appreciation Card from the deck of twenty-seven cards, then followed the instructions on the card. Lastly, we recorded our experiences and what we learned on an *Appreciation Experience Form.*

We hope that these examples give you a good idea on how to use this exercise to increase your love and appreciation for the life we live in the human body. Do this exercise as you are drawn to it, or as a part of your plan for angelic enlightenment. Designing a plan for enlightenment is discussed in more detail in chapter 30.

May the energy of the Archangel Uriel assist you to complete the integration of your self-segments and lead you to a fuller appreciation of love and beauty in all its aspects.

Heaven is inside you right now, because
the grace of God lives within you now.

365 Days of Learning and Appreciation
Appreciation Experience Form—Peter's Experience

Date: **2-6-98**   Time: **6:00 p.m.**

Card Topic: **Writing**   Card Number: **14**

Instructions: **Write a letter to a loved one. Imagine that loved one is no longer on this earth. Say all your heart would long to say.**

What did you experience during the exercise?

I experienced some tensions & feelings of anger and jealousy towards the other person. I allowed myself to write down all the hurt I had felt since I knew that I wouldn't be actually mailing this letter in its original state. I also experienced other positive feelings which I had felt when I was younger with this person.

What did you learn to appreciate and why?

I learned that it can be difficult to move past layers of old hurt. These layers seem to cloud the original states when there was a balance in the relationship—no matter which kind of relationship. I have come to appreciate the process of exploring my past hurts because I believe they are leading me to a point of self-forgiveness & forgiveness of others. I appreciate the opportunity to heal & the ability to realize that I need to heal. I learned to appreciate my shadow-self and to see its function as one of self-protection from pain & rejection.

365 Days of Learning and Appreciation
Appreciation Experience Form—Linda's Experience

Date: 1-20-98   Time: 2:15 pm.

Card Topic: Eyes closed   Card Number: 1

Instructions: Blindfold your eyes for one hour. Use your hands to feel & your ears to listen. Do This in the middle of the day if possible. For safety have a partner nearby.

What did you experience during the exercise?

I first noticed the absence of light & lack of visual stimulation. I wondered— what can I do for the next hour? I can't read at all or write very well. Then the phone rang— I managed to answer it on The 2nd ring & wrote a message for Peter while blindfolded. I had to Trust my memory & hope the letters formed words. Then I decided to listen to T.V. Geraldo was on — I found I didn't wAnt to listen to his show if I didn't have any visual cues. I ended up listening to a sermon and Then the Rosary recitation. I noticed That I "heard & comprehended" a lot more Than when I "watch" T.V.

What did you learn to appreciate and why?

I first appreciated my hands, which helped me to "feel" my way around The house. I then appreciated my legs & feet which carried me carefully around the house. With no visual cues, I found that I listened with more care and with all of my energy centers (chakras) open & sensing. I listened more with my heart & less with my mind. I was less analytical & critical of the words being spoken. I was able to feel the vibrational power & message of the Rosary as well as the care & intent of the speakers. The words seemed to penetrate & cleanse my chakras. This "listening with care" led me to a more loving & giving state. I felt an appreciation for the abundance in my life as well as a desire to give.

A Plan for Angelic Enlightenment

A person is disposed to an act of choice by an angel . . . in two ways.
Sometimes, a man's understanding is enlightened by an angel
to know what is good, but it is not instructed as to the reason why . . .
But sometimes he is instructed by angelic illumination,
both that this act is good and as to the reason why it is good.

—St. Thomas Aquinas

26

Ethics and Angelic Enlightenment: Creating Your Personal Guidelines

AS A PART of humanity, we each have the spark of divinity within us. We've already written about various ways to help keep this divine spark alive and growing within us: prayer, meditation, and the techniques and powers of the four Archangels. But there is another powerful gift we can give ourselves, our loved ones, and the world. This gift involves the clarification of our own personal code of ethics.

Ethics are the principles and values that we use as guides and standards in our personal decision making. Most of us already, albeit unconsciously, follow an internal code of ethics that we probably learned from our parents, friends, and cultural norms. The gift that we can give ourselves and the world is to make this internal code a conscious code of personal ethics.

Why would you want to create your own personal code of ethics? Because defining your own personal code of ethics will help to harmoniously balance your inner world and your outer life.

Writing down our personal guidelines or philosophy helps to develop, define, and protect our personal integrity. In this process, the lost or hidden talents and resources we possess become uncovered, then unified and finally strengthened as we consciously align our outer, everyday world with the reality of our inner spiritual nature.

As we come to know and trust ourselves, the beauty of our inner spiritual nature begins to shine through our hearts. In turn, this beauty lights our path. Let us call forth this light by consciously invoking all that is good and grace-filled within us! Harmony and peace fill our being as we unite with the light of our inner spiritual nature. Our eternal and everlasting oneness with ourselves and God is then restored. It has been there all along, waiting, as we process and heal the painful scars that had only temporarily obscured the beauty within.

Examples of Codes of Ethics

Our everyday outer life is made up, in part, by choices we can make consciously or unconsciously. Let us choose consciousness. Let us choose integration, wholeness, and love. With this in mind, we will share with you our personal code of ethics. We each keep our list of ethics taped to our bathroom mirror as a daily reminder and affirmation of the world we strive each day to consciously create and live.

Linda's Personal Code of Ethics

1. Today, and always, I choose to actively envision a positive attitude toward life. Today I will find at least one positive thing to say about any challenging situation I may encounter. I will articulate my honest feelings about the situation and consult my inner self, asking "What is there in this situation that will stimulate growth?" I will ask for help and share any insights with my partner. I will affirm, appreciate, and promote the positive qualities I see in all beings and situations around me.

2. Today, and always, I choose to tell the total, complete truth to myself and to those in my world. I will truthfully share my feelings in a positive, constructive manner. I am truthful in spirit, word, and deed, and I feel the wonderful alignment of energy within me as I truly live this way more and more each day.

3. Today, and always, I choose to fully feel, appreciate, and honor my feelings for what they have to teach me about myself and my world. I am grateful for the experience of being human, of being alive.

4. Today, and always, I choose to listen with my heart, without interrupting. I allow others to tell me the truth of who they are and what they feel. I strive to listen and speak without judgment or censure.

5. Today, and always, I choose to look inward for guidance, inspiration, and messages from my higher self—to bring this wisdom into manifestation in my physical life and in fulfillment of my life's mission; to pay attention to my dreams; to move toward alignment with my soul self; and to seek integration, unity, and oneness with God and all creation.

6. Today, and always, I choose to acknowledge all responsibility for my behavior and actions; I choose to create an appropriate response to all situations I encounter.

7. Today, and always, I choose to believe in and love all parts of myself, the known and the unknown, the inner and the outer, the reality and the potential, without reservation and with my whole heart. I choose to believe in the potential and goodness of all human beings.

8. Today, and always, I choose to follow my inner vision and move forward in my life, in fulfillment of my life's mission. I commit to moving forward with my husband toward goals that are mutually creative and fulfilling. I commit to ask him and others for support when I feel alone and overwhelmed.

9. Today, and always, I choose to promote the health and well-being of all those whom I come into contact with, in particular with my husband Peter and our children; to enrich their lives and support their growth with the love and vision of all that is good within me.

10. Today, and always, I choose to enjoy whatever it is I am doing; to have fun and to find meaning and contentment in all my daily activities.

Peter's Personal Code of Ethics

1. I strive daily to keep my heart open to the spirit of life. To allow myself to feel all that I am feeling. To resist instinctual reactions that influence me to cover up and hide. To honor and respect all beings—friends and strangers.

2. I strive daily to learn more about my own motivations. To learn how I have contributed in fashioning my life as it is today and to find ways to improve and change. To achieve an alignment with my soul's purpose and pattern.

3. I strive daily to share more of the being who I am. I will be a willing conduit of the life force. This means allowing my energy centers to spin freely—to be themselves.

4. I strive daily to express myself more clearly. This will help me and those around me. By expressing myself more clearly, I assist others. They can understand me better and respond from a position of truth and knowledge, avoiding confusion and misunderstanding.

5. I strive daily to support my loved ones and friends. I support them in word, thought, and deed, with encouragement and with self-honesty.

6. I strive daily to bring humor and lightness to life. To use my intellect and the wisdom of my higher self to bring calm and to make the way here easier.

7. I strive daily to take steps toward accomplishing my life's mission. To listen to the guidance of my soul self and the Archangels. To move forward when I am too tired to move forward. To take a chance to fall when I am afraid to fly.

8. I strive daily to process the repression of my past. And I try to keep from adding more unprocessed emotions to my "pressure cooker" by expressing in the present to the best of my abilities.

9. I strive daily to accept the experiences of my life. To allow myself to feel the pain so that I may feel the fullness of the love. To accept the goodness and to embrace the difficult.

10. I strive daily to Be.

No two people are exactly alike, nor do they have the same issues in this lifetime. Thus, each person's personal code of ethics will be different as it reflects their uniqueness, creativity, and personal growth issues. Our prayer is that you will take the time and effort to create your own personal code of ethics which will, in turn, help you in achieving harmony and balance between your inner and outer worlds.

We hope you find this information useful in constructing your own personal philosophy and guidelines. Feel free to create a shorter or longer list as your needs dictate. Linda has revised her list several times in her life as she worked through personal issues and new ones emerged—so don't be afraid to add and delete as time goes by and new arenas of growth and discernment enter your awareness.

As we evolve, so does the whole world evolve,
for we are all connected, hand to hand, each to the other,
by the unity of our divine nature.

27

Understanding Your Dream Symbols

EVERYONE DREAMS. WE may not always remember our dreams but as we mentioned before in the section on our "spiritual toolkit," we need to dream in order to maintain proper health. Dreams are a window to understanding ourselves and the purpose of our individual existence. One of the most important purposes of dreaming is to heal—to heal our relationships with ourselves, with our loved ones, and with those who have passed on to the spirit realms. At the end of this section, we will give some pointers on how to remember your dreams.

Dreams are direct channels which, if properly interpreted, lead us to our soul self and to a deeper awareness of our mission for this lifetime. They connect us to our creative energy and often provide solutions to problems that elude our waking consciousness. The vast majority of our dreams involve our dream self seeking to unite and integrate our physical, emotional, mental, and spiritual selves. Their purpose is to heal painful traumas and relationships by giving voice to the parts of our psyches that have been repressed or denied expression in our everyday lives.

For example, since infancy we have learned to protect ourselves by "killing" off parts of ourselves that we felt were unacceptable to our loved ones. We need to reclaim these lost parts of ourselves, understand them, and heal them. We meet these lost parts of ourselves in our dreams.

Ultimately, the most important person we have to forgive is our own self, and dreams provide an excellent forum for self-understanding, forgiveness, and growth.

Dream study has been around for thousands of years—there are multiple examples of this kind of study in the Bible. One of particular interest is from Job 33:14–16. It reads:

> *For God speaketh once, yea twice, yet man perceiveth it not./ In a dream, in a vision of the night, when deep sleep falleth upon men, in slumberings upon the bed;/ then he openeth the ears of men, and sealeth their instruction.*

Thus, dreams not only connect us to the various lost parts of ourselves, but they also provide a connection for God to communicate with us, to support us in living a more loving and responsible life.

Dream Symbol Analysis

Dream symbol analysis is not as simple as a dream dictionary might lead you to believe. "A" does not always equal "B." For example, if you dream about water, it usually indicates the emotions. But sometimes it does not. Depending on the dream context and your own individuality, water could symbolize a need for physical cleansing; thoughts or portents of death (as in a wide river); or even a literal, impending flood in the basement of your home.

Keeping the above in mind is just as important in dream analysis as knowing yourself and your issues in this lifetime. As we become more conscious of who we are and of our patterns of reaction/response, we can determine the most likely interpretation to a dream. For example, one theme in Linda's life has been an internal struggle between a strong need and desire for independence and the flip side of this—a fear of dependence. Armed with the knowledge of her issues, Linda can look for possible amplifications and solutions to this struggle within her personal dream symbology.

There are no trivial dreams. Even the most silly-appearing dream has an important message for you. In fact, our dream-maker often uses humor to capture our attention. For example, have you ever had a dream where you had to go to the bathroom very badly, but despite a long search you either could not find one or when you did find one you could not relieve yourself because it was filthy, or it was simply a stool set in an open area with no walls and you had to use it in front of everyone, or all you could find was a bathroom meant for the opposite sex? This is a very important, common dream that usually signifies a need for physical cleansing, dietary changes, or a need for greater water intake to flush the impurities out of your body. We would do well to listen to the messages from our dreams—they could help us avoid, for example, damage to our kidneys, liver, or pancreas.

Thus, you see that our dream-maker is always trying to promote our health—the health of our physical, emotional, mental, and spiritual bodies. Why does our dream-maker use such hard-to-decipher symbols? Because that is the universal language of our collective unconscious, of our personal unconscious, of our higher self, and of our soul self. You have heard the saying that, "one picture is worth a thousand words"; so too do dream symbols allow multiple complex ideas to be communicated to our conscious, waking self in a single dream. Thus, dreams enjoy a universal language that transcends, and is not limited by, diverse cultural barriers, great distances, and space/time conceptualizations.

In addition, dreams also have a wonderful capacity to present to us multiple layers of meaning that can be uncovered with each new stage of growth throughout our lifetime. For example, a childhood dream can be re-analyzed periodically throughout our lifetime as we grow and learn more about ourselves, our issues, and our personal patterns. We can apply the light of our wisdom gained from life experiences and increased self-knowledge to early traumas, recurrent nightmares, or messages we may not have fully understood.

To illustrate this, Linda would like to share with you a recurrent, early childhood dream which she has re-analyzed periodically throughout her life. She calls it her "lion" dream, and although nothing horribly scary happens in it, it frightened her enough as a child to label it a recurrent nightmare. First, a word about nightmares. Nightmares arise from a very primal part of our unconscious self. They are a sign that our inner pain is reaching a pressure point and is demanding attention, now!

Psychological wounds are real, and the nightmare is trying to provide information to the conscious self. When examining these dreams, be very gentle with yourself. Don't tell yourself you are wrong for how you feel about the dream. Most importantly, don't ignore your nightmares and hope they go away. There are many levels, or layers, in our dreams, and it takes work to figure them out. As mentioned above, it sometimes takes years for all levels of meaning to be realized from a single dream. Be patient and diligent in your dream study, and you will be rewarded with deep insights about yourself and your life journey.

L I N D A ' S   L I O N   D R E A M

An Analysis

The dream consisted simply of me becoming aware that there was a large lion sitting in my bedroom closet, looking at me with huge, yellow eyes. As a child I thought this meant only that I was terrified of lions, as are many children. I did not understand dream symbology at all then, and so I did the only thing I could think of to reduce my fear—I read about lions and wrote a report about them for a class assignment.

A few years later, I realized that I was afraid of what this lion represented. But I wasn't sure what it represented. Did it represent strength, or courage, or . . . ? Later still, I realized the lion represented the animal, or beast, part of my nature. But what part of my animal passions did it represent? I knew lions to be ferocious and protective of their young. I knew, from my earlier report, that lions lived in families called prides. I still wasn't sure. So I finally asked myself a very important question. What part of my nature was I most afraid of?

I still wasn't sure what I was most afraid of. Then I looked at the rest of the dream; the context and the dream setting. The lion was sitting passively in my closet, not threatening me—yet I was terrified of him. This led to the next level of interpretation as I realized that the thing I was most afraid of was my own anger. Anger can wound if it is expressed inappropriately; lions and anger both have teeth and claws that can tear and rend people if allowed to. As a child, I did not have the skills to appropriately express or even identify my anger. My dream was trying to help me. Thus, it was only years later that I realized the lion represented my anger, and that I had tamed my anger (note that the lion was sitting passively in the closet—waiting to express itself but unable to). As a child, I held my anger in because I thought it might hurt and alienate others, like my parents and friends. Letting my anger out of the closet would certainly hurt me. I believed that if I let it out, it would attack my parents and thus they would not love me as much.

You can see that throughout the years I have continued to work on this dream and finally allowed it to help me see a pattern within myself. By being patient and keeping my attention on my dreamscapes, I was able to put the insights together, one by one, over the years, until I had finally completed the puzzle of this dream. It has been of tremendous value in my interactions with others to be aware of this tendency or pattern to hide my anger from myself and others. I still am not done with this dream.

Only recently I have realized how much this pattern of hiding my anger cuts into my personal energy, my personal strength, and my personal courage. No longer do I choose to sacrifice any part of my lion's strength, courage, or energy. I strive daily to use my lion's courage in appropriately identifying and expressing my anger to myself and to my loved ones.

Each successive dream interpretation level or layer builds upon and enhances the prior one. We are building a dream vocabulary unique to ourselves. As we do this, it can be beneficial to learn some of the universal themes or symbols that can be found in our dreams, as long as we remember that "A" does not always equal "B" and that these symbols can and do have multiple meanings. In other words, don't jump to conclusions. Always correlate any universal symbology with your own personal dream vocabulary as well as with the self-knowledge you have gained about your tendencies, patterns, and early traumas throughout your life.

If you have a dream that seems to defy interpretation, spend some time closely examining the current situations in your life. Take a look at any recent problems that you might be struggling with. Make note of any unusual events that occurred in your life within the last few days. Your dream may be trying to provide you with clues on how you're feeling inside (about a particular situation) as well as solutions to a current problem you may be faced with.

Common Dream Themes and Symbols

The following list highlights some of the dream themes and symbols that we have found helpful in interpreting our dreams and the dreams of others. The following list is not intended to be a complete list of all universal dream symbols, rather it is a list of the few we have found to be the most typical and reliable when interpreting our own dreams.

There are many dream dictionaries available at book stores, but personally, we feel these dictionaries tend to confuse rather than clarify since each seeker is a unique individual and has their own symbology. This personal symbology can only be discovered through knowing ourselves and our significant issues. Of all the books and authors we have studied, we have found the Edgar Cayce books on dreaming to be the most helpful in the realm of understanding dream symbology.

The most important thing to remember in dream study is that the dream characters almost always represent a part of yourself or a quality within yourself. We will explain more about this later. What follows are some common, universal symbols and their usual meaning:

Amount of light or darkness within the dream: The amount of light or darkness within a dream represents the amount of conscious awareness we have of the issue presented in the dream. For example, if our dream setting is very dark, or if we can't see at all, we would assume that we are dreaming about something that we have little or no conscious awareness of.

Animals within dreams: Animals usually represent part of our beast or animal nature, meaning not just our sexual passions but also our need to protect and nurture our young, to provide shelter, etc. Animals can also serve to represent a certain quality within your dream—for example, a horse might represent fleetness or strength, or freedom, or the desire to escape a situation. It depends on the context of the dream and how you relate to the particular animal.

For example, do you like horses or are you afraid of them? What experiences have you had with them that might color your perceptions and feelings about that particular animal? Linda loves horses and, in fact, she had a palomino that she absolutely adored when she was young. Thus, when a horse appears in her dreams, it usually represents the quality of beauty and strength within her. If the horse happens to be sick, then she knows that something in her life situation is cutting into her strength and the way she views herself. She determines what this is by the dream context and how she relates to the horse and the other characters in the dream. Always ask yourself, "What quality within me does this animal represent?"

Attic: The most conscious part of yourself, sometimes your higher self. If your dream takes place in the attic, anyone you may meet there will probably be bringing you information from the wisdom aspect of your higher self. Attic may also mean memories or the wisdom gleaned from past experiences.

Basement: The unconscious mind, the basic self. It includes the things we have repressed or hidden from our own awareness (e.g., early traumas, and "guilty" memories). However, the basement can also represent the gateway to our collective unconscious.

House or home: These elements usually represent you, your personality, or your bodily needs. In the dream context, the room you find yourself in indicates what part of yourself you are trying to understand or work with. For example, if one is in the basement in their dream, it would probably indicate that they are working on some part of themselves that they have little or no conscious knowledge of, such as a buried or repressed trauma. If they are in the bathroom, it would likely indicate a need for internal cleansing; likewise if they were in a bedroom it would indicate an issue with intimacy, sexuality, or a need for rest.

Nudity: Nudity usually means that you are feeling exposed and vulnerable in some area of your life. However, if you enjoyed the experience of being naked in the dream, it could indicate an openness to new experiences or a shedding of inhibitions.

People we meet in dreams: These usually represent an aspect or part of yourself that is similar to that person. For example, if you dream about having an argument with a friend, this would probably indicate that you are really having an internal struggle with the part of yourself (or quality within yourself) that is similar to a quality that you consciously recognize in your friend (it is likely to be a quality or characteristic that you don't want to admit you have or are feeling).

Water: In most cases, *water* signifies the emotions. For example, if you are dreaming of a tidal wave, it could mean you are feeling overwhelmed by conflicting emotions. Depending on the dream context, water could also indicate a need for internal cleansing or greater water intake, or possibly a literal flood in your basement. You need to look at your current life situation, the context of the dream, and any feelings or fears you may have about the situation being presented to you.

The above examples should give you a general sense of how to look at the characters and creatures in your dreamscapes. By remembering that most things in your dreams are parts of you, you can also figure out what the activities that take place in your dreams mean.

For example, if you are being chased in your dream, you can safely assume that there is a part of yourself that you are afraid of; a part of yourself that you are running away from or do not want to acknowledge. If the figure you are running away from is an unknown male, it could indicate that you are afraid of part of your masculine nature. Similarly, if the activity apparent in your dream is eating, this indicates that you are taking in something, perhaps knowledge or wisdom of some sort. It could also be a warning about needed dietary changes—only you can decide for sure because you know yourself and your situation better than anyone else.

Dream Dialoguing

Another helpful technique in dream study is to create an imaginary dialogue between yourself and the dream characters. This extends not only to the people and animals in your dream, but also to inanimate objects such as containers, windows, trees, tables, or utensils. For example, if you dreamed about a red flowerpot, ask that flowerpot some questions: "What are you trying to tell me?" "What are you made out of?" "How does it feel to be a flowerpot?" "Why are you red?" "Why aren't any flowers growing inside of you?" Answer the question as if you were the flowerpot. The idea is to take the point of view of as many of the characters in your dream as possible and have them engage in dialogue with you and each other in order to get as much information from them as you can.

These symbols are all parts of yourself that need to be heard, expressed, and integrated. They come to us in symbolic form because that is the rich language of our subconscious self. Finally, if one or more of these symbols are huge (like an unrealistically huge flowerpot the size of a house), this means it is a very important symbol for you to analyze and that your subconscious is going to extremes to tell you it is an urgent issue for you to deal with.

More rarely, we sometimes have dreams that represent actual communications with either a deceased individual or a spiritual being from other realms, such as the angelic realms. These dreams are marked by their clarity and vividness. Usually there is an important message that the being or deceased relative wishes to impart, and if it was a true visitation, the message will be positive, healing, and helpful to you and to the world. Sometimes the deceased relative simply wishes you to know that he or she is well and thriving in the next world. You will usually notice that this person is glowing with health, and looks years younger than when he or she passed away.

Remembering Your Dreams

As we have said—everyone dreams. If you are having trouble remembering your dreams or believe that you do not dream, review the following chart. It outlines a few simple techniques to help you remember your dreams.

Dream Remembrance Hints

1. **Get enough sleep.** If you need to, go to bed early.

2. **Give yourself a pre-sleep dream suggestion.** Say to yourself at least three times in a row: "I will remember my dreams when I wake up."

3. **Get a dream journal.** Keep it, along with a pen and a flashlight, beside your bed each night. You can also use a tape recorder if you prefer.

4. **Upon awakening, move your body as little as possible.** Record your dream, or if it is still in the middle of the night and you are too tired, write down some key words or symbols. These will help trigger your memory of the dream in the morning.

5. **Find a friend who is also interested in dream study.** This is someone to share your dreams and techniques with. This will reinforce your commitment and it will tell your subconscious that you are interested in the information it has for you.

6. **Write in your journal.** Note any questions or concerns you would like your dream-self to help you with. Create some possible conscious solutions to these problems and see what your dreams tell you about the issue(s) that night.

7. **Re-create the dream in reverse.** Sometimes we can only remember the last scene in a dream. Think about the last scene you remember and ask yourself, "What happened before this?" In this way, we can successively trace a dream's events moving backwards from the end toward the middle, and then to its beginning scene.

8. **Keep a written record of your feelings, daydreams, and fantasies.** This tends to encourage and stimulate your dream-maker.

9. **Be patient.** What you give attention to will bear fruit. This is ever true of your dreamworld as well.

Dreams are experiences to learn from and to grow by. Learn to interpret your dreams. This ability will benefit you throughout your life and provide you with insight when you most need it. The Archangels and your soul self are sending you their help when you most need them. Look to your dreams for understanding and direction. They will point you in the direction of wholeness and the love that is within you.

Pleasant Dreams!

*Dreams are direct channels, which, if properly interpreted,
lead us to our soul self and to a deeper awareness
of our mission for this lifetime.*

28

A Guide to the Emotions

FEELINGS AND THE deeper emotions that lie beneath them are part of our heritage as human beings. They are gifts to us that tells us, in part, who we are in this lifetime and who we have been in past lifetimes. We carry with us, from one lifetime to another, an emotional blueprint colored by a unique pattern of reacting and responding that is apparent in our personality even in early infancy. How many times have you heard a mother say that each of her children exhibited markedly different and unique personalities from early on? Even in the case of identical twins, this has been evident. Thus we are often described as, "she was a very quiet baby, undemanding and peaceful," or, "she needed constant reassurance as a baby, otherwise she would cry, fidget, and scream for no apparent reason."

Our feelings give color to our world; they give voice to our perceptions about ourselves and of the world around us. If we don't have an awareness of what our feelings are and of what they mean, we lack a real awareness of life itself. If we rationalize or intellectualize away our feelings, we run a high risk of living a deadened and distorted life. Our feelings may make us uncomfortable at times, but they are our friends in truth because they tell us where we're at, they stimulate growth, and they make us aware of a need for change because something is not right in our world.

This emotional blueprint colors our aura and influences every detail of our multiple lives in a cumulative manner. The emotions are neither negative nor positive; remember, they are indicators that tell us what is happening within ourselves. They also tell us what is or is not "right" in our world. They should not be ignored, hidden, or repressed. Pushing our feelings down throughout our lifetime can lead to patterns of depression, disguised anger, low energy, deep sadness, and even illness.

Part of the task in living a more conscious life is to pay attention to our feelings as they occur and to resolve any repressed traumas, confusion, or painful events we may have experienced in our life thus far. This will help to clear our energy fields so that space is created for spirit to fill with the divine grace of God. This grace forms a bridge to the wisdom of our higher self, which in turn is then free to promote personal growth and the evolution of our being. As we evolve, so does the whole world evolve, for we are all connected, hand to hand, each to the other, by the unity of our divine nature.

How do we express our feelings with honesty and without harming others? This is where the L.E.A.R.N. technique is helpful. It teaches us, first of all, how to label and identify our feelings. Many of us unconsciously repress our feelings because we haven't been taught how to identify them.

Our parents were unable to teach us because they had never been taught themselves. We didn't learn how to say, "I'm mad at you because . . ." or "I'm hurt by . . ." or "I feel worthless when . . ." Instead, all we learned was an inner feeling of frustration that we could not put a name to. We learned to feel shame and not know why. We learned to be quiet when our parents yelled at us to "behave now, or else!" We learned how to hide parts of ourselves that we felt were unacceptable to our parents, to our friends, and to the world.

We may not have learned how to express our happy and joyful emotions, either. We may never have heard or been able to say, "I feel happy when . . ." or "I feel proud when . . ." Some of us have never heard our parents say the actual words, "I love you." Thus it is difficult for us to know if we love, or whom we love, or how to express feelings of love, joy, and appreciation. Therefore the first task is to learn how to label and identify our feelings.

To assist you in this process, we have developed a list of emotions along with a simple, clear definition for each. You can use this list anytime you find that you can't quite name precisely what it is you are feeling. You can also use it to clarify unexplored or repressed feelings you may have experienced from some earlier trauma in your life.

For example, we may wish to take a look at some abandonment issues we might have from earlier in our life. Maybe one of our parents died, or maybe our parents just weren't emotionally available for us at one time or another during our childhood.

When this happens, a part of us is hurt deeply. We may not have even admitted to ourselves how badly we were hurt. We may have been taught to be stoic or tough on ourselves by being rewarded for not showing our feelings. Even our culture works against us by its unwritten code that one should not be overly emotional or overly affectionate. This creates within us fear of showing our feelings and leads to even deeper stoicism.

Some cultures promote the healthy expression of feelings, and consequently enjoy lower rates of suicide, depression, etc. For example, bereaved families in Middle Eastern cultures customarily wail, cry loudly, sob, and moan publicly at their loved one's wake. This healthy expression of deep grief is frowned upon in our society. Instead, we sit quietly at our loved one's funeral, holding our grief within us, unable to share our sorrow except in silent tears. Many of us aren't even able to discuss our feelings of loss in private with family members. We're told, "be strong, things aren't so bad."

During this process of healing, we need to learn to re-parent ourselves. We do this by working actively with our feelings in a kind, gentle, and loving manner. We tell ourselves (in our imagination) that it's okay to have these feelings and to express them to ourselves and others in appropriate ways.

Below is a list of feelings and emotions that we all, as human beings, experience to some degree in our lifetime. They are what make us human. Sometimes people have learned to harbor odd notions about their feelings. They may fear that if they admit to being anxious or angry about something, others will think they are weak or unspiritual. Be alert for this possible tendency within yourself—in actuality it is those people who know themselves who are full of strength. To know ourselves we must figure out and be honest about what we are feeling. This is real courage.

The list that follows can be helpful in clarifying any confusion whenever you can't quite describe exactly what you are feeling. You can also use this list each evening during the nightly review to make sure you haven't unconsciously repressed some feelings from that day, to help you define what exactly you were feeling.

One feeling can often trigger another feeling. For example, a feeling of guilt can often trigger anger because we may be feeling guilty about forgetting something (like an anniversary). We project our anger onto our partner by saying something like, "You know how busy I am. Why didn't you remind me?" By projecting the fault onto someone else, our feeling of guilt is lessened, at least for the moment.

A vicious cycle of blame and projection has begun. Instead of projecting we could have simply expressed the truth: "I feel guilty for forgetting. Will you please forgive me?" The guilt/anger cycle is ended by being honest and taking responsibility for our action of forgetfulness.

The Two Main Groups of Emotions

Emotions fall into two main groups. All center around the divine quality of love. The first group, as shown on the chart below, are emotions that reflect the acceptance of love in our lives. The second group are emotions that reflect the fear of losing love. Remember, emotions are neither wrong nor right. They are clues for helping us to learn more about who we are.

Love	
Emotions that reflect the acceptance of love	**Emotions that reflect the fear of losing love**
appreciation	anger
contentment	anxiety
courage	depression
humor	fear
joy	greed
love	guilt
wonder	sadness
	shame

Emotions That Reflect the Acceptance of Love

Appreciation

Appreciation is a state in which your heart is opened to life. By appreciating something or someone, you are increasing that object or person's value in your life. Appreciation is the flow of energy from you to others that accepts them as they are; it is the seeing of the divinity within each being and form and object; it is to respect all forms of creation with care and concern.

Low intensity	Appreciation		High Intensity
thoughtful	honored	grateful	compassionate
	sympathetic	thankful	reverent

Contentment

Contentment is a state of balance where each energy center (chakra) is spinning in alignment with our knowledge of soul's pattern and purpose. It is to be in harmony with the divine plan and the ebb and flow of the universe. It implies fullness and is akin to joy. One emotion sparks another. Contentment leads to joy, and joy to an all encompassing love for all life.

Low intensity	Contentment		High Intensity
relaxed	gratified	heavenly	serenity
relieved	protected	peaceful	
satisfied	secure		

Courage

Courage is a state that reflects our commitment to the divine plan as it relates to our soul's purpose and our life's mission. To have courage is to accept the dispatch of Gabriel and commit to carrying it out to the best of our abilities, no matter what hardships we may encounter. Courage is trusting in the goodness of life and of God. Courage is accepting our fear and injecting it with the love of the soul self.

Low intensity	Courage			High Intensity
hopeful	determined	confident	bold	brave
optimistic	energized	proud	decisive	noble
	inspired			

Humor

Humor is a state in which we are able to turn suffering into learning and pain into love. We take the hardships of daily living and look at them in various ways to help us gain a greater appreciation of the human experience. Humor engenders a love for the little things in life and brings a lightness to living that helps us by releasing tension. Humor is useful in dislodging ourselves from narrow viewpoints.

Low intensity	*Humor*		High Intensity
amused	funny	jovial	hilarious
light-hearted	jolly	mischievous	
	playful		

Joy

Joy is a state marked by bursting energy that begins in the solar plexus center and moves up quickly into the heart center, spreading the feeling of intense happiness and love of living. It is a state where we look forward with anticipation to tomorrow and the experiences of life without fear of loss or pain. It is a state where the soul self can be heard singing a song of love for God and for its eternal existence throughout all worlds and universes. Joy is experienced when we, as the conscious self, have the experience of the awareness of the soul self.

Low intensity			*Joy*		High Intensity
pleasant	cheerful	happy	enthusiastic	thrilled	blissful
	delighted	merry	excited	triumphant	exhilarated
					ecstatic

Love

Love connects us to the wholeness of life itself. It is much more than a passing feeling. Usually centered in the heart chakra, it brings a feeling of warmth that begins in the heart center and spreads throughout the body. Love is a bond of care and concern for ourselves, our children, parents, friends, the world, the Angels, and all beings in all worlds of God. It is the essence of life. It gives life its greatest meaning and has influenced men, women, and nations since the dawn of time. It is the root emotion that all other emotions either reflect acceptance of or reflect a fear of losing. Love is the motivating force. It is the catalyst that sparks all growth. It is the first power that emanates from the God-head and moves throughout all the universe. It is God's energy calling us homeward. It is the pure spirit of the Creator that nourishes each of us. In it we find our growth and in it we find ourselves.

Low intensity		Love		High Intensity
kindness	affection		cherishing	passion
	warmth		tenderness	rapture
	caring		wholeness	

Wonder

Wonder is a state wherein we realize the beauty of life itself. We see life's intricate design and focus on what a miracle it truly is. Wonder is a state that leads to joy and joy to love. Wonder is a state where we are impressed by the immensity of creation and the role that we play in the endless drama of life as each day unfolds before us. It is a state of deep insight, for we are looking beyond the surface experience to appreciate existence itself.

Low intensity		Wonder		High Intensity
curious	surprise	enchanted	amazement	awe
interested		fascinated	astonishment	

Emotions that Reflect the Fear of Losing Love

Anger

Anger is a strong feeling of displeasure caused by a real or imagined injury and is often accompanied by a desire to take vengeance or obtain satisfaction from the offending party. Anger turned inward upon oneself (feelings of hurt and frustration that are not expressed) can turn into a state of depression.

As a state of pain, anger comes from our internal conditioning, which links our expectations and the experiences of life to our ability to accept and give love. Sometimes anger may be an explosive feeling of rage and betrayal; or anger can be milder, such as a feeling of irritation because someone said something that disappointed you. Many small disappointments could build up into simmering or smoldering feelings of resentment and hostility. People often get angry when they feel hurt, and so whether we realize it or not, we all feel angry at times. Anger comes from losing the ability to love according to our internal belief systems.

Low intensity		*Anger*		High Intensity	
disapproving	grumpy	aggravated	bitterness	aggression	fury
exasperated	huffy	obstinate	cheated	betrayed	rage
irritated	sulky	stubborn	contempt	hateful	
perturbed		thwarted	disgust	hostile	
			resentment		

Anxiety

Anxiety is a feeling of apprehension surrounding a fear of being hurt or of losing something. Whether the fear is real or imagined, it feels the same. Extremes range from mild apprehension to a state of panic. The energy of anxiety is initially centered in the third-eye/crown chakras, then moves into the solar plexus and heart areas. If left unchecked, it intensifies and can lead to desperate and irrational behavior that clouds the perceptions. It is the opposite of acceptance.

Low intensity		Anxiety		High Intensity
concerned	confused	dismayed	anguished
fretful	nervous	hysterical	desperate
perplexed	sick	pressured	insane
puzzled	tense	stressed	
restless	worried		

Depression

Depression is a state of sadness characterized by a loss of interest in usual activities, fatigue, changes in appetite and sleep habits, feelings of worthlessness, and suicidal thinking. It includes self-condemnation and can represent a pattern of reaction involving a withdrawal from life. It can also represent a reaction to real or imaginary losses in life. If real, the place to begin is to give yourself permission to grieve; feel your sadness and write down these feelings. Talk to a therapist or friends. Expressing is the beginning of healing. If the loss is imaginary, look at the secondary triggering emotions and follow them to the root emotion—the truth of the situation.

Depression is also a state of sadness usually caused by deep repression, which manifests as the inability to fully express pain. Marked by the loss of the ability to love, depression is a serious state. Many people deal with this issue daily. Depression can make a sunny day gloomy and life itself to seem like a prison. Afraid to love, the depressed person spins an ever-deepening cycle of isolation from the heart center.

Low intensity		Depression		High Intensity
bored	blue	depressed	alienated	helpless
lazy	isolated	empty	burdened	powerless
tired	moody	indifferent	defeated	suicidal
trapped	mopey	withdrawn	despondent	worthless
			lonely	

Fear

Fear is a state of turmoil that ranges from mild timidity to extreme horror. Fear is the root emotion of all other emotions in this section. It is the base emotion linked to the loss of love. We, as the conscious self, have forgotten our eternal nature. Therefore, we have the belief that love will be taken from us through others, our own actions, or by death. The most basic instinct for survival is to maintain consciousness. The fear of death (the loss of consciousness) is the fear of the loss of acceptance and love. In the case where death is believed to be the final door of life, the conscious and basic self may interpret death as the ultimate act of rejection. This rejection is assumed to be a rejection of the self as a being. Not knowing what to do, the self becomes unable to function. Fear is the opposite of courage.

Low intensity		*Fear*		High Intensity
bashful	disturbed	alarmed	frantic	horrified
hesitant	doubtful	frightened	nauseated	petrified
shy	suspicious	threatened	panicked	shocked
timid	vulnerable			

Greed

Greed is a state of imbalance where the energy centers are constantly taking in, but not returning, the flow of love into the world. Instead of love, a flow of will is moved through the energy centers, particularly the third eye and crown centers. To be in a state of greed to is to be afraid of losing material forms and substances. The material form and substance are seen as permanent and non-changing, therefore of value. This is an illusion that the conscious self accepts. The reality is that the forms and substances are forever changing and the desire to hold on to the form and substance in its current state is an unwillingness to accept the design and flow of life. Greed is the opposite of the state of appreciation. Where in appreciation we give value *to,* in greed we take *from* life and give no value back.

Low intensity		Greed		High Intensity	
dissatisfied	spoiled	arrogant	deceitful	spiteful	envy
	selfish	obnoxious	lecherous	two-faced	jealousy
		stingy	sneaky		

Guilt

Guilt is a state where we are conscious of breaking a code of ethics or a rule accepted by the soul self to follow and live life by, and in the process we devalue ourselves. To feel guilt is to know that we have done something that has either hurt ourselves, or another, or both. It is a state of self-condemnation where we shun ourselves as unworthy. Guilt reflects a fear of the loss of love because we are afraid to admit to the truth of our actions.

Guilt is the feeling that we have made a terrible mistake; we have done something wrong. Feelings of chronic guilt can lead to shame. "I did something bad *(guilt)*; therefore I am bad *(shame)*."

Low intensity	Guilt	High Intensity
apologetic	culpable	ashamed
embarrassed	contrite	immoral
foolish	regretful	remorseful
inadequate		sinful
mistaken		

Sadness

Sadness is a state in which we feel the pain of life. It is less debilitating than depression, for we are still able to express our pain when experiencing sadness. Because we are able to express the pain, we are able to move deeper to accept love. Sadness can be a state in which we do not accept life's design and we wish for things to be different. When we feel sad, we have forgotten the eternal nature of the soul self and the goodness of the Creator. Sadness is a fear that we may never feel joy and love in the area that we are sad about. Sadness is the opposite of joy.

Low intensity		*Sadness*		High Intensity
apathetic	exhausted	gloomy	abandoned	agony
disappointed	ignored	miserable	lonely	grief
discouraged	melancholy	pained	sorrowful	mournful
				tortured

Shame

Shame is a state akin to guilt, but much stronger. It is a state where we wish to have no consciousness rather than to be aware of what we have done. It is a state where we condemn ourselves as unlovable—both to ourselves and to the world. To that end, shame reflects a deep fear not only of the loss of love in the present, but the prospect that we may never be worthy of love or able to love in the future. We feel that our very being is corrupted and totally unworthy of love or respect. Shame is a state of self-loathing sometimes associated with a "loss of face."

Low intensity		*Shame*	High Intensity
embarrassment	ashamed	pitiful	humiliated
inferiority	bad	rejection	worthless
		self-condemnation	self-loathing

Dealing with your feelings is what makes you feel alive!

29

Motivating Yourself on
Your Journey to Enlightenment

IN PREVIOUS CHAPTERS, we have focused on formulating our personal ethics, understanding our dream symbols, and expressing our emotions. We now come to the task of finding ways to motivate ourselves as we move toward enlightenment.

What is Enlightenment?

Enlightenment is the state we reside in when we have come to "know ourselves." It is a state of soul-infusion where all segments of the self are integrated and in union with the divine energy of God. Through the application of the principles discussed in the preceding chapters, we will be able to uncover our personal truths, heal our pain, and chart a new course for our lives.

The moment "now" is the singular moment of truth for each one of us. It is the moment when we can realize the full impact of our personal situations and accept rather than deny our place in the universe, as a human being, as brother, sister, father, mother, as a temporary resident of the planet earth. We will know that we are living in the moment when we experience the radiance of the Holy Spirit permeating our being.

When we are immersed in the moment, we seem to be flowing within a stream of divine energy down a river of endless life into a sea of God's love and mercy. All of our cares, worries, and concerns are in their rightful places. And all of our shields, barriers, and masks are lowered. In order to reflect the light of God, we must reveal our true selves to that light.

During the times when life challenges you—the times when you want to give up—there paradoxically exists the very real opportunity to propel your growth beyond normal daily boundaries. It is at these times that the core issues that affect you, your unfoldment, and enlightenment are at their apex. Be courageous. Use these windows of opportunity to propel your growth. Life will end someday and you will be left to sift through the experiences and wonder what life could have been if you had only . . . ?

A Life Review

This short exercise can help you gain a perspective beyond the consciousness of your ordinary day-to-day routines. When you move your awareness to a new vantage point, you can trigger the growth of the seeds of wisdom within you. It is as if you have moved from the shadows into the light of the sun or allowed the rain from the sky to pour its enlivening resources upon you.

E X E R C I S E

Life Review

Relax in an easy chair or lie down on a bed. Make yourself comfortable and close your eyes. Next, imagine that the day of your death has arrived. In whatever form this time has come—through old age, accident, or disease—see yourself leaving your body and this world behind. Imagine that you are traveling up higher and higher in the atmosphere above the earth. From this vantage point, the earth is seen as a sphere suspended in blackness. You find yourself in a room. There is another presence in the room with you. You do not know this other presence, but it is familiar and supportive. You relax in this room.

Next, within a large window opened to the blackness of space, images begin to appear. These are images from your lifetime on earth. These images are for you to view and learn from. Using the image window to review your life, perform the following steps:

1. Ask for an image to form that shows a significant event in your life. Do not dictate the event. Simply ask and then wait for the image to form. When it does, view it and re-experience it.

2. Next, ask yourself if there are any regrets that you still hold about that particular event. Is there anything that you would have handled differently now that you know that you live after the death of your body? What different choices would you like to have made knowing that your life on earth was but a temporary sojourn?

3. Lastly, imagine and see—through the image portal—the reaction of life and how events around you would have been had you chosen other courses of action and behavior. "See" the results of those changes and how they would have affected your life and the lives of others—both friends and adversaries.

Perform the above steps on three separate events from your lifetime. When you are finished, thank the presence beside you. It is your soul self. Gently open your eyes and return to waking consciousness. Reflect on this exercise.

How do you want to look back on this lifetime when it is completed? What will fill you with pride and what will fill you with regret? Take the time now, while you are here, to ensure that when you leave this world your legacy will be one that you can feel good about, and that your only regrets will be that you could not do more good and for a longer period of time!

The Motivational Power of Miracles

For centuries, men and women have searched for signs from life, nature, and God to prove the existence of life after death. Will our pain and sorrow someday be lifted? Many miracles have been recorded in holy books and the journals of saints, seekers, and holy men. Some miracles are astounding, while others contain a simplicity that belies their importance. In each case, the miracle could be viewed as a wondrous event. How many of us have not yearned at some time in our lives for a sign or mira-cle from something beyond ourselves to show itself to us and guide us?

Miracles can motivate us to renew our commitment to continue on the path of self-mastery by reminding us of the wonder of life itself. Miracles stir the waters of our heart so that we reconnect with our desire to grow and learn. They offer proof to our basic and conscious selves that the eventual demise of our body does not mean that our individuality will vanish as well.

LINDA'S STORY

Finding Meaning in Daily Events

Finding meaning within the daily events of my life has been the most powerful factor in strengthening and maintaining a positive, motivated attitude. There are many ways to create meaning in our lives. I would like to share what I have learned about this with you.

Since my own early childhood, my mother's deep faith and personal testimony has been an important source of hope and inspiration for me. She taught me to always look for the miraculous within my daily life—this included viewing dreams as signs and sources of wisdom. Every morning we would share our dreams with each other and look for the most likely meaning.

Mom sometimes had prophetic dreams. For example, every time she dreamed about going blueberry-picking (once or twice per year) she would discover that a friend or family member had passed away or was ill and would shortly pass away. She viewed this dream as a helpful forewarning, a sort of mental and emotional preparation that to her was not at all frightening or negative. Perhaps this was because she viewed death as a "coming home" wherein we are reunited with our deceased family members and friends. Although she herself recently passed away into the spirit realms, her inspira-tional stories survive to remind us to always look for meaning, and even the miraculous, within the seemingly simple events of our daily lives. I would now like to share with you one of her stories.

My mother's biggest passion was her garden. Or I should say, her gardens. She always had two huge vegetable gardens and several flower gardens that she planted, weeded, watered, and harvested nearly single-handedly. She loved to tell the following story:

"It was the hottest, most humid August day that I can remember. The air was totally still, stifling—I felt almost breathless. I had been weeding and thinning the carrot patch for over an hour, and I knew I should work on the onion row as well. Sweat was streaming down my forehead, I was sticky all over. Something had to change! So I called on my deceased and beloved brother Leo for help, saying out loud, 'Leo, send me a breeze!' and immediately, to my relief, a wonderful cool breeze sprung up and enabled me to complete the gardening work I had planned for that day."

This is just one of the ways that she taught me to look for signs and to ask for help from family, friends, or angels in the spirit realms. To some this might seem like a lucky coincidence, but to her it held meaning beyond the physical relief it gave her. It meant that sometimes our prayers are heard, even in mundane matters. To her, it supported her belief that her brother Leo could hear her supplications and even intercede on her behalf at times. Finding meaning in daily life occurrences confirmed her faith and helped her sustain a hopeful outlook even in difficult times.

It takes time and practice to learn to recognize and trust our intuition. In addition, we need to become familiar enough with our own personal symbols to correctly interpret the signs and messages coming to us from our higher self, the dream worlds, and the spirit realms.

Another way that my mom gave meaning to her life was to do something each day to serve others and to let them know they were important to her. To her this meant baking or cooking special foods for family members or neighbors. She would often call us up on Friday evenings, wondering if we were planning on coming home to the farm that night. She would tempt Peter and me by letting us know that she had a fresh batch of homemade vegetable soup cooking on the stove, and that it would be ready in a couple of hours—just the length of time she knew it would take us to drive up to the farm.

Cooking and baking were my mom's way to give, and it was also her primary creative outlet. She indulged this creative urge by baking nearly every night, sometimes well past the midnight hour. When we would try to encourage her to go to bed and get some rest (she was battling ovarian cancer), she would answer, "Not yet. I have to finish baking this apple pie for our neighbor, John. He doesn't get anything homemade since his wife passed away and I know he'll be wanting something 'good' to eat."

Many of us have been fortunate enough to have a mother, an aunt, or grandparents in our lives to nurture and serve us in the manner my mother did. However, in the current generation, many women work outside the home and simply don't have the time or the energy to bake or cook into the wee hours of the morning. Yet the need to serve and nurture still exists—for both men and women—and it is beneficial if we can find ways to fulfill this need to give to others.

I like to nurture Peter by writing him little love notes and leaving them as surprises under his pillow and also, in the manner learned from my mother, by making him a salad nearly every night. This makes him happy and it also gives me an opportunity to indulge my culinary creativity. Thus, serving others (even in small ways) fulfills two functions—it helps us to find meaning in our own lives and it can be a creative outlet for us. We need to nurture our creativity in some manner each day. By doing this, we keep an open line to the energy of our soul and to all that is good within us. Indeed, this inner good is strengthened each time we choose to give creatively.

Sources of Inspiration

Hope is the feeling that enables us to believe that change is possible for us within our lives and within our hearts. To stimulate motivation and hope within ourselves, we need to discover who and what is our source of inspiration. In short, as human beings, we need heroes. Who is your hero? Think about this. It is one of the most important keys to developing and maintaining motivation.

Below is a summary of ideas that can help you to discover your own source(s) of inspiration, hope, and motivation:

1. Learn to recognize and understand the signs from your higher self as they appear within your dreams and in your daily life experiences.

2. Write down these signs and dreams. You may discover a pattern or important messages within them.

3. Share your dreams and signs with a trusted friend. They can help you sort out possible meanings and help you make connections to current life situations which you might have missed on your own.

4. Figure out who your heroes are. They may be saints, mystics, or miracle workers such as Padre Pio or Mother Teresa. Spend time appreciating their inspiring qualities.

5. Find a way to serve others each day. This will strengthen your connection to your inner "goodness" and it will help you find and maintain meaning in your daily life.

6. Indulge your creativity. This is your lifeline to the energy of your soul.

Your Personal Miracles

Take a few moments now to consider the miracles, great or small, that you have experienced in this life. Write down five miracles that you have experienced in your lifetime in the lines below. It may be hard, but try to pick at least five "wondrous" events from your life. This may require you to view your past experience in new ways. Later, during your meditation or contemplation exercises, focus on items from this list to re-experience the gratitude and awe that the original experience brought you. In this way, you can draw from the power that the original event brought to you and apply it in your present life situations.

1. _____

2. _____

3. _____

4. _____

5. _____

The Angel's Pool: A Time for Healing

After this there was a feast of the Jews, and Jesus went up to Jerusalem. Now there is in Jerusalem by the Sheep Gate a pool, which is called in Hebrew, Bethesda, having five porches. In these lay a great multitude of sick people, blind, lame, paralyzed, waiting for the moving of the water. For an angel went down at a certain time into the pool and stirred up the water; then whoever stepped in first, after the stirring of the water, was made well of whatever disease he had.

—John 5: 1–4

The Angel's Pool

Relax and sit in an easy chair or lie on a bed. Close your eyes and imagine that you are at the pool called Bethesda. There are many people gathered, all waiting to descend into the pool to be healed. Move to the steps that lead into the pool and wait. After a few moments, the water begins to stir. You walk down the steps and enter the pool of water. The pool is shallow enough for you to touch the bottom with your feet and still keep your head above the water. You are now standing in the center of the pool.

As the water continues to swirl around you, feel it enter your heart and gently stir the energy centers, soothing and healing unresolved conflicts, fears, and anxieties. Feel the desire to live and participate in your life arise from within the core of your being.

Stay in the pool for as long as feels comfortable, soaking in the healing and strengthening currents. After a few minutes, thank the Angel of the pool for the opportunity to refresh yourself. You are now enlivened to complete the tasks that you have chosen in this lifetime. Open your eyes and return to waking consciousness.

Using Imagination to Motivate Yourself

Another powerful method of motivating yourself to continue toward your goal of integration and enlightenment is to use your imaginative powers to create the space for your goals to be realized. Do you recall the segment on daydreams from chapter 4? In that segment, we explained that daydreams are experiences and that we use the techniques in the toolkit of angelic enlightenment to process those experiences. Allowing yourself to believe in possibilities is of crucial importance in opening to an experience. So you ask, "How can my imagination motivate me?"

By imagining what your life will be like after you attain your goals, you set up the canvas for that experience to appear—in other words, you create the environment for your imagination to paint on the canvas of your life. Rather than waiting for something "to happen," you have modified the energy streams and channeled them into pathways for change.

Visualize all that will occur when you define and accomplish your life's mission. Observe how your completed mission will affect those people you know and those you do not yet know. Imagine how it will affect you personally. How will you feel when you successfully embark on your journey and begin to see the fruits of your labor manifest around you? As you practice using your imagination in this way, you are releasing energy and adjusting its vibration. This released energy will affect everything around it by the principle of displacement.

Whenever you feel powerless, use your imaginative faculty. This God-given tool is available to all and can help you lift your spirits and continue to deeper levels of connectedness and spiritual union. It has been used by saints, sages, masters, and holy men throughout the centuries when they have faced challenges in life—and you can use that same spiritual tool in your world today!

Creativity is the lifeline to the energy of our soul.

30

Creating an Angelic Enlightenment Plan: A Guide to Integration and Self-Mastery

THE FIRST STEP in creating your plan of angelic enlightenment is to determine the amount of time you have available to devote to it each day. We suggest that you set aside about ten minutes each morning before your work day begins to do a short invocation or prayer addressed to the Archangel you wish to work with on that particular day. This will help you consciously open to the inspiration and guidance of your chosen Archangel. The energy stream distributed by this Archangel will then be available to you throughout the whole day.

As you go about your day, be alert for new ideas, signs, and guidance that might be flowing to you from the Archangel(s). This guidance will always be positive, helpful, and healing for you personally, as well as for humanity as a whole. You will find it helpful if you keep a small notebook with you to jot down any thoughts or ideas that occur to you. A sentence, or even a single word, can trigger recall at a later date when you have more time to fully examine and develop the ideas. The more you nurture your creativity, the more it will flourish. The attention you give to your spiritual nature will also enhance your connection to the energy streams of the Archangels.

If you feel negativity or anger spinning within you, it is likely that you have not fully acknowledged the hidden repressions or expressed the pain of a past or current situation in your life. You will want to call upon the Archangel Raphael to help you work through these feelings in order to uncover the root emotion. Refer to chapter 28 to trace and define the path of repressions to the root source (i.e., in what way are you afraid of losing love in this particular situation). As outlined in the L.E.A.R.N.

technique, by fully processing our feelings and emotional states we create the space within ourselves for God's grace to fill. This grace brings with it renewed energy, creativity, and the ability to define and complete the purpose of this incarnation— our life's mission.

After your workday is completed, we suggest that you set aside about one hour each night to practice the techniques and meditations of the Archangels. This will help you to fully develop any inspirational ideas you may have had during the day. As you work toward enlightenment (integration) and self-mastery, you learn to appreciate the human condition more fully. Your compassion and desire to extend yourself to help others expands because you are infused with the knowledge that we are all part of the same universal human condition. It becomes clear to you that we all face the identical task of integrating ourselves—within the parameters set by the challenges and opportunities inherent in our diverse life circumstances.

Love, Wisdom, and Power

LOVE: Love comes into your life because you choose to give and receive it by immersing yourself in life through integrating all the segments of the self.

WISDOM: Wisdom comes into your life by using the fuel of experience to propel your growth through the stages of life and integrating the lessons for future use.

POWER: Power comes into your life by taking responsibility for your choices and circumstances. It is the ability to change the values and beliefs and attitudes that you hold. This enables you to gain the experience that you desire.

Simply put, the more love you give, the more you receive. This pipeline of consciousness is enlarged by giving, thereby enabling us to accept more love in return. By taking responsibility to look deeper at the choices you have made and are making in life you become a more honest and loving individual.

As you remove the vestiges of incorrect thinking and false assumptions that have masked the understanding of the true causes of your experiences, a renewed hope and love for life enters your heart. Even though the pain of your past experiences may be difficult to view, your choice to honestly and openly explore how you have fashioned your life will help you heal and find new meaning and purpose.

The commitment to viewing your role in creating your experiences—good or bad—will come in varying degrees depending on what you want in the moment. Your level of commitment is based on your desire to face the self that you may have been denying. Consider this: Look inside yourself right now. Take a moment. Ask yourself what you are aware of in your life that you know you should take care of but are ignoring. Be honest with yourself. Isn't it your choice to not pursue this important issue in your life because it may be too painful (for various reasons) to confront? Or perhaps you feel that there is not enough to be gained by pursuing this particular issue. Understanding your childhood conditioning can help you remove blocks to your energy and awareness. Working through painful issues helps you to identify your patterns of conditioning. A clear understanding of how this conditioning has contributed in forming your values and beliefs is paramount to your taking the initiative to change your future experiences, your destiny, and to achieve self-mastery.

Recovering all the parts of yourself takes effort, determination, and commitment. Call on the Archangel Gabriel to strengthen your courage and commitment. If needed, give yourself small rewards for achieving goals along the way. We have also found that it helps to make a specific and measurable commitment to something or someone outside of yourself. This could be a partner, trusted friend, or a cause to which you are devoted. In this way, you add more importance to reaching your goal.

Remember, life on earth is a constant rearranging of the energy of God; the One Energy. Sometimes we feel content to allow only the One Energy to move us. While it is true that we do move with the energy and current of life itself, we must also do our share. We need to participate in our lives to the extent that we can and are able. Step by step, at our own pace, we need to take action to unlock the blocks to our vital energy so that we can create and manifest all that was intended for us in this lifetime.

Life is a Balance

If you are feeling overwhelmed in your efforts, take a break. Take time off from the pursuit of your goals and just be. Life is a balance. When we have had enough of a break, we will instinctively choose to resume our efforts. The cycles of effort and rest are a part of the rhythm of being a human embodied on the earth plane. They are a part of the human experience. Be good and kind to yourself and to others. Allow yourself room to grow and to make mistakes. Allow the same for others as well.

Sometimes prayer and meditation can help you when you are looking for direction. In the case where you feel that you have waited and rested long enough, you must begin to make proactive movements. These movements rearrange the One Energy. Forms and substances will change around you based on your movements. This action alone has the power to break a spiritual stalemate and give your unfoldment a kick-start. When you are tired, rest; when you are weak, gain strength; and when you are full of energy, create and manifest that which you desire.

Appreciation Gives Value and Meaning to Life

Being too close to something for too long can cause us to not see the forest for the trees—to take for granted aspects of our life. If this is the case, try the 365 Days of Learning and Appreciation exercise with the Archangel Uriel. This exercise can help you recharge yourself and learn to understand the value of the forms and substances around you. It will assist you in developing an attitude of charity toward yourself and others, and it will also help you learn to cherish the God-given qualities within yourself and others.

If you are in a state of confusion arising from a situation that is full of emotion, try Raphael's L.E.A.R.N. technique. It can help bring clarity out of the strong and confusing currents that the emotional self is presenting to us for our attention. Sometimes a situation can drain us of our power because we are unsure of how to proceed. We find that this lack of power manifests as an inability to act. The L.E.A.R.N. technique can gently move us to action again.

Change is Movement Toward Growth

Try the Charting Your Life exercise from Archangel Michael. Use it to identify values and beliefs that are moving your life in a particular direction. By changing these attributes, you change your attitude and therefore your direction of travel. This is an excellent way to move the energy toward change and growth.

And finally, Gabriel's Creating Change exercise would be very useful in taking a step, any step, no matter how small, in changing a current energy flow. Miracles occur as the energy of God changes within and without us. Create change in your life in a loving and supportive way.

Motivating yourself to self-mastery, like other things in this life, is an ongoing process. Just as interest compounds in a saving account, so too does the effort you place toward attaining enlightenment compound the spiritual accomplishments within you. In other words, life *does* get easier as you grow spiritually because you are working along with life and not against it. By exercising your will to live purposefully you increase your ability to meet life's challenges. You grow in the attributes of strength and personal courage.

The Next Step

Armed with this knowledge and the guidance of the four Archangels you are ready to create and follow a plan to angelic enlightenment. What are the components of a good plan? Included here is a sample plan that you can use as a template for your own:

1. **Read and study *Angelic Enlightenment: A Personal Process.*** Contemplate any concepts that you are having trouble with and view them from various angles. If the concepts do not ring true to you, do not modify your beliefs to fit the concepts. The ideas are not dogma. Your truth lies in being who you are. The world is waiting to see *you.*

2. **Start each day with a prayer to the Archangels.** Use the prayers to set the tone for the day or to remind yourself of the guidance of one or more of the Archangels. You can say the prayers anytime during the day. Morning and night are good times to say the prayers, for it is then that you are just coming out of and going into the sleep state. During these times, you are naturally in a more receptive state to the other self-segments.

3. **Perform one of the exercises of the Archangels.** Use one of the techniques inspired by the Archangels. Use the one that you are gravitating toward or feel would help you in your current situation. Sometimes it is hard to start the exercise process, but you will find that you will gain energy by your willingness to focus on growth and learning. You can do an exercise daily, or use one of the meditations contained in this book. If your schedule is busy, or you are tired, you need not perform the exercise that day. Remember, we use these exercises as tools—they are not duties to perform.

4. **Give yourself time and space to grow and learn.** Reading and performing the various exercises is important because they can help you to focus on growth, and give you new viewpoints to explore. But, in and of themselves, reading and performing the exercises alone will not lead to enlightenment. What leads to enlightenment is experience, processing, and integration. This is where we learn the truth of ourselves. Put down all reading material and exercises and just live! SEE . . . FEEL . . . ACT . . . BE! The materials and exercises are tools to use when you need them. They are not the goal. For example, the question to ask yourself is not whether you did a meditation today but rather, what did you learn about yourself during that meditation.

5. **Write down your thoughts and feelings.** Keep a journal of your thoughts and feelings. Purchasing a new journal to mark the beginning of your journey can serve as a symbol of your dedication and commitment to the process of integrating your self-segments. Some people prefer to carry a microcassette recorder. In either case, any time that you are opening to knowledge from your soul and higher self, it pays to record it on paper or tape. Very often, thoughts from the inner realms are fleeting. We may think we will remember them, but as quickly as they came, they are gone. Write them down, write them down, write them down! They are messages from your inner self. Read them and contemplate them. Often they will lead you to more information from yourself than you knew you possessed.

6. **Write down your dreams and learn to interpret them.** The benefits of processing your dreams has already been covered. If you wake with a dream that you feel has deep significance for you, try to take the time to write it down on paper. Often while writing down the dream, more segments of the dream come to your awareness. You can interpret the dream right away or set it aside until another time. If you are pressed for time, just write down a single word or image from the dream. You can then use this word or image to trigger your memory when you have more time to recall and process the dream.

7. **Read an inspirational book or article.** Sometimes it helps to step back from our own lives to learn from the experiences of others. It can be inspirational to examine the lives of people who devote themselves to improving the quality of human life. Despite adversity, persecution, and sometimes lifelong

illnesses, these people somehow find the strength within themselves to go on; to continue to trust in God; to give meaning to their lives; and to selflessly serve others. They have been called many things—saints, mystics, holocaust survivors, and war heroes.

Their life stories can inspire hope within us. The flame of hope is kindled within us as we study the attributes—both human and divine—of these unique individuals. If you read their autobiographies, you will see that these individuals suffered the same doubts as we do. They had fears and human failings that they struggled with daily just as we do. Some of the most inspiring are the Holocaust survivors. Somehow, despite their ordeals, they still believe in the goodness of God and humanity. The lives of such people are often filled with mystery and miracles. Miracles do happen. Study the miracles of the Saints—and be alert to the miracles occurring within yourself and within the lives of those around you.

8. **Carry with you a reminder of your divine purpose.** This could be something you carry with you (like a prayer card) that you keep handy in your pocket, wallet, or purse. It could be a picture of a loved one or a saint—someone whose attributes you admire and strive toward. It could be a symbol or a picture of a goal that you wish to achieve. It should be something that holds special meaning for you. It could be something you wear, such as a special necklace or crystal.

LINDA'S STORY

Integrating Enlightenment

When Peter and I got married, we wanted our rings to signify our divine union in the universal Christ. So, with this in mind, we chose matching wedding rings on which the Christian cross was formed from a pattern of small diamonds. Each day, whenever we touch or glance at our rings, we are reminded of our love, of our divine union in Christ, and of the purpose of our lifetime together.

The symbol or message you choose should serve as a reminder of your divine purpose. It could be something as simple as a single statement, personal affirmation, or famous quote that you find inspirational. You will want it in a form small enough to easily carry it with you. If it is made of paper, you might want to laminate it to keep it from fraying.

These are just eight possible ideas for developing and implementing your plan. You will think of more as your plan evolves. For example, you may wish to study with the Archangel Michael for a period of three months, then move to Raphael for three months, Gabriel for three months, and then Uriel for three months. During each three-month period, practice the exercises and work along with that Archangel's power and purpose. Gather many views about the Archangel in question. Read all that you can about him. Accept only what feels right to you. Examine it fully, then discard the rest.

With the information given within these pages and your earnest effort to change and grow, you can become more honest, heal your heart, choose and complete your life's mission, and come to appreciate the love and beauty of all creation. Good luck on your journey and may the Archangels and Angels guide and inspire you always.

Experience is the fuel that propels our growth.

Appendices

And I saw another angel flying through the heavens,
carrying the everlasting Good News
to preach to the people who belong to this world—
to every nation, tribe, language,
and people.

—Revelation 14:6

Appendix A

Glossary of Angelic Enlightenment Terms

THE FOLLOWING DEFINITIONS are here to assist you with terms that may be unfamiliar to you as they are used in this book.

Acceptance: Taking responsibility for the choices we have made and viewing ourselves with truth and honesty. Acceptance is one of the three main attributes of Archangel Raphael.

Affirmation: A statement or phrase repeated verbally or internally to oneself that helps to reinforce positive patterns and constructive beliefs within the self-segments.

Angelic beings: Known as messengers of God, the Angels are a parallel evolution to humanity. They are the builders of form and hold the matrices of energy for all life forms on earth (including the plants, animals, humans, and the Earth itself). The Archangels are at the top the Angelic Hierarchy, and because of this responsibility, they are very concerned with building unity between all life forms and the Creator. The Angels are light beings who are also in the process of evolving. They are intricately involved with the care of the Earth and all its inhabitants. They work hand-in-hand with humanity, inspiring us to create as they build and hold together the energy matrix for God, humanity, and all life forms on planet Earth.

Angelic enlightenment: A state of soul-infusion in which all segments of the self are integrated and in union with the divine energy of God. States of bliss and loving compassion for all of humanity are a part of angelic enlightenment. Creativity and productivity are natural by-products of angelic enlightenment because as one's chakras become open and balanced, the divine energy of God and the inspiration of the Angels are able to flow through them. One then has access to formerly blocked energies.

Archangels: The Archangels are beings of light and pure spirit. They exist naturally in a state of divine grace and unity with God. They wish to share this state with us. They are the Cardinal beings through which the main energy streams of God are channeled to the universes. Throughout all time, they have been charged with the divine mission to inspire, protect, and guide humanity in our journey here on the earth plane.

Archangels' Plan of Healing: A plan that combines the unique purpose and power of each of the four Archangels (Michael, Raphael, Gabriel, and Uriel). The Archangels' plan initially inspires humanity toward integration of our self-segments, and ultimately toward the awareness of divine union with God, the Angels, and all of creation.

Aura: The energy field that surrounds all animate and inanimate objects and beings. The aura can be seen, heard, and felt by those who are sensitive to the inner energies or who have trained themselves to achieve the necessary level of sense perception.

Awareness: The perceptions of energy streams. The integrated knowledge of past, present, and future experience. A modifiable state under our control. What we focus on is brought to our awareness.

Basic/Subconscious Self: The survival self that watches out for our immediate interests, as well as that part of the self that urges us to view issues that we as the conscious self have chosen to repress.

Beauty: The sensation of completeness of a form, whether composed of physical matter or the grouping and order of experience. The manifestation of the One energy that touches the core of the soul. Beauty is one of the three main attributes of Archangel Uriel.

Chakras: An Eastern religious term used to denote the various energy centers within the physical and etheric bodies. Chakras can be viewed as wheels that process energy in and out of the body form.

Collective unconscious: The concept that humanity has a group consciousness that is continually growing as each being experiences, then processes those experiences. The collective unconscious contains archetypal symbols that are universal across human cultures.

Commitment: The attribute that describes the decision of the self to follow an agreed upon process to its completion. Commitment is one of the three main attributes of Archangel Gabriel.

Conditioning: A process which links one action or energy force to a reactive action or returning energy force. Conditioning can be positive (for the individual's growth) or negative (causing us to react in unconscious, repetitive, non-productive patterns).

Conscience: The small, still voice within us. The whispering of the soul self. The awareness of soul's plan and purpose.

Consciousness: The fundamental state of awareness where we have the ability to process experience.

Conscious self: The ego self known as the waking self or the personality. The state we most identify with in our day-to-day life.

Contemplation: Viewing concepts and situations with the inner virtual domain of the imagination.

Detachment: Accepting the current situation and reality of our life in the present moment.

Desire: The magnetic force that calls us to the source of our being. Desire is the source of all growth. It is intertwined with experiencing the earth world.

Emotional Self: Part of the self that reacts to life's experience to provide us with vital clues in an effort to remain open to the heart center.

Energy: The essential substance of all life.

Entrainment: A scientific term that describes the process of aligning the brain wave frequency within a specified bandwidth.

Etheric body: Subtle body of non-physical nature that helps to process divine energy to and from the physical self.

Ethics: A set of rules or guidelines that an individual can choose to live their life by.

Experience: Slices of life that carry the vibrational imprint of all levels of our awareness at a specific time.

Gabriel: The Archangel who distributes the divine attributes of strength, persistence, and commitment. Gabriel is well-known as the Archangel who gave the divine dispatch to Mary that she would bring into the world the Christ. Gabriel's main power is to act and his main process is accomplishment.

Guided meditation: A meditation that is facilitated by another person. This facilitation can be verbal or written.

Honesty: The divine attribute that reflects the complete expression and truthfulness of what we are experiencing and have experienced within ourselves. Honesty is one of the three main attributes of Archangel Michael.

Healing: The process of resolving discordant energy streams skewed by fear, incomplete processing, and lack of expression. Healing is one of the three main attributes of Archangel Raphael.

Higher self: The wisdom pool of each soul, which contains the knowledge and wisdom of all soul's experiences.

Holy Spirit: The essence of the Creator. Also known as the life force.

Inner child: Part of the self that is connected at all times to a state of wonder about life itself. It can also refer to a part of us that was wounded at an early age—a part of us that continues to need nurturing.

Imagination: God-given faculty that allows us to work with divine energy in order to experience and learn within a safe, protected environment.

Justice: The acceptance of the cycles of experience that we have chosen. Justice is one of the three main attributes of Archangel Michael.

Karma: The cycle of experience as chosen by the soul self.

Love: A state that connects us to the wholeness of life itself. It is much more than a passing feeling. Love is a bond of care and concern for ourselves, our children, parents, friends, the world, the Angels, and all beings in the worlds of God. It is the essence of life.

Manifestation: The state in which our creative choices are made evident to ourselves and to other beings.

Meditation: Temporary stilling of the mind to allow access to other thought streams and vibrations.

Michael: The Archangel whose divine attributes are truth, honesty, and justice. The leader of the Archangels. Michael's main power is seeing, and his process is understanding. The first step within the Archangels' plan of healing is under the direction of Michael.

Mirror of Truth: Symbolic mirror in which the self-segments have no option but to see and recognize themselves and their actions.

Past life regression: A facilitated experience where one is guided into a state of connectedness with one's own higher self. During a regression, the soul self sends images from the wisdom pool of the higher self to the conscious self for use in current life situations.

Persistence: The state where energy is applied over time in a recurrent fashion. Persistence is one of the three main attributes of Archangel Gabriel.

Power: The ability to act. This includes the ability to feel, to express, to manifest, or to see.

Prayer: A method of communicating with our inner self, the Creator, and other beings.

Projection: The experience of viewing the truth of your internal alignments of energy within other beings, as if they were mirrors of yourself. For example, when we are uncomfortable with a particular feeling and cannot admit to having it, we often project that feeling onto others and accuse them of having that particular feeling.

Raphael: The Archangel whose divine attributes are healing, wholeness, and acceptance. The patron of travelers. Raphael's main power is feeling and his main process is expressing. Raphael is well-known for his healing abilities as portrayed in the story of Tobias's journey in The Book of Enoch.

Reincarnation: Belief that the soul continues to extend itself into the worlds of matter, energy, space, and time for the purpose of experience (i.e., multiple lifetimes).

Repression: Refusing to express the actual vibrational reality of our reactions to life.

Strength: The increase of one's power within a specific area. Strength helps one to accomplish their goals and is achieved over time through the application of energy in a repetitive manner. Strength is one of the three main attributes of Archangel Gabriel.

Soul: The imperishable self composed of pure spirit.

The Sword of Truth: A symbolic sword that is used to slice through the self-made barriers of illusion that one has placed around one's self.

Truth: The expression of universal and personal awareness to its deepest levels. Truth is one of the three main attributes of Archangel Michael.

Uriel: The Archangel whose divine attributes are love, beauty, and awareness. Uriel holds forth the flame of love within the palm of his hand to all who wish to learn. His main power is being and his main process is appreciation. The guidance of Uriel completes the cycle of growth with the Archangels' plan of healing.

Wholeness: A state associated with acceptance and healing and which indicates an integration of all aspects of our experiences. Wholeness is one of the three main attributes of Archangel Raphael.

Wisdom: The processed and integrated experiences of our life.

Appendix B

Expansion Sheets for Personal Use

EXPANSION SHEETS ARE included in this appendix for you to use to perform the various exercises in *Angelic Enlightenment: A Personal Process.* Copy these sheets for your personal use as you follow the book. Included in this appendix are expansion sheets for the following exercises, which are presented in full throughout the book. The Angel Cards for completing the 365 Days of Learning and Appreciation Exercise are printed on cardstock and bound into the end of this book.

1. Charting Your Life: Subject Scale
2. Charting Your Life: Events and Observations (side A)
3. Charting Your Life: Events and Observations (side B)
4. The L.E.A.R.N. Technique: Discovering the Root Emotion
5. The L.E.A.R.N. Technique: Nightly Review
6. Creating Change Summary
7. Creating Change Detail Sheet: Side A
8. Creating Change Detail Sheet: Side B
9. 365 Days of Learning and Appreciation

Charting Your Life
Subject Scale Sheet

Date: _____   Time: _____

Subject: _____

Scale 10:   _____

Scale 1:   _____

```
10

 9

 8

 7

 6

 5

 4

 3

 2

 1

     1    2    3    4    5    6    7    8    9   10   11   12

    __   __   __   __   __   __   __   __   __   __   __   __

    (----------------------------  time / date  ----------------------------)
```

Note: The numbers on the left of the graph relate to the scale as filled in at top. The numbers at the bottom of the graph are time/date slices. The lines under each time/date slice are for you to enter the time and/or date that the number represents (i.e. 1 = Jan 98, 2 = Feb 98, etc.).

Charting Your Life
Events and Observations: Side A

Date: _____   Subject: _____

_____

Event 1 notes

_____

Event 2 notes

_____

Event 3 notes

_____

Event 4 notes

_____

Event 5 notes

_____

Event 6 notes

_____

Charting Your Life
Events and Observations: Side B

Date: _____   Subject: _____

_____
Event 7 notes

_____
Event 8 notes

_____
Event 9 notes

_____
Event 10 notes

_____
Event 11 notes

_____
Event 12 notes

_____

The L.E.A.R.N. Technique
Discovering the Root Emotion

Date: _____   Time:_____

Describe what happened:

1. Label: Identify your initial feelings (anger, rage, jealousy, etc.) and write down as many statements as you can that describe these feelings.

2. Express: Write down the feelings (pain, disappointment, hurt, rejection, fear, etc.) that are underneath the first layer of feeling that you identified in step 1.

3. Accept: Write down the feelings underneath the pain and fear in step 2 (guilt, regret, ownership of your own feelings and the part you played in helping to create the situation).

4. Release: Write down the feeling underneath the regret and guilt from step 3 (love, appreciation, forgiveness, and hopes for the future).

The L.E.A.R.N. Technique
Nightly Review

Date: _____   Time: _____

1. Describe the event and what happened.

2. What are your main feelings about the event?

3. How did you handle the event, what did you do?

4. How would you change the way you handled the situation?

5. Develop a plan to amend the situation.

Creating Change
An Exercise with Gabriel
Change Summary Expansion Sheet

Date: _____   Time: _____

        Task To Accomplish   Need Level Completed

1. _____   _____   _____

2. _____   _____   _____

3. _____   _____   _____

4. _____   _____   _____

5. _____   _____   _____

6. _____   _____   _____

7. _____   _____   _____

8. _____   _____   _____

9. _____   _____   _____

10. _____   _____   _____

Creating Change

Steps to Change Detail Sheet: Side A

Date: _____   Time: _____

Task To Accomplish: _____

Describe accomplishing the task

_____

_____

_____

_____

_____

Your Positive Affirmation of Accomplishment

_____

_____

_____

_____

_____

Creating Change
Steps to Change Detail Sheet: Side B

Step	Order	Completed
_____	___	___
_____	___	___
_____	___	___
_____	___	___
_____	___	___
_____	___	___
_____	___	___
_____	___	___
_____	___	___
_____	___	___
_____	___	___
_____	___	___
_____	___	___
_____	___	___

365 Days of Learning and Appreciation
Appreciation Experience Form

Date: _____   Time: _____

Card Topic: _____   Card Number: _____

Instructions: _____

_____

_____

What did you experience during the exercise?

_____

_____

_____

_____

_____

_____

What did you learn to appreciate and why?

_____

_____

_____

_____

_____

_____

Index

Archangel
URIEL

*365 Days
of Learning
& Appreciation*

Archangel
URIEL

*365 Days
of Learning
& Appreciation*

Archangel
URIEL

*365 Days
of Learning
& Appreciation*

Archangel
URIEL

*365 Days
of Learning
& Appreciation*

Archangel
URIEL

*365 Days
of Learning
& Appreciation*

Archangel
URIEL

*365 Days
of Learning
& Appreciation*

Archangel
URIEL

*365 Days
of Learning
& Appreciation*

Archangel
URIEL

*365 Days
of Learning
& Appreciation*

Archangel
URIEL

*365 Days
of Learning
& Appreciation*

1. Eyes Closed

For the period of one hour, blindfold your eyes. Use your hands to feel and your ears to hear. Do this in the middle of the day if possible. For safety, have a partner or helper nearby to avoid any accidents if you choose to move about.

2. No Hands

For the period of one hour, do not use your hands for any function at all. Do this in the middle of the day if possible.

3. No Legs

For the period of one hour, do not use your legs to walk. Do this in the middle of the day if possible. You may crawl or creep.

4. No Talking

For the period of 24 hours, do not use your voice to communicate in any way. You may use written communications.

5. Hearing

For the period of one hour, place cotton in your ears or wear ear plugs. This is to deaden sounds around you.

6. Listening

For the period of one-half hour, go out into nature and write down all the sounds that you hear. Relax.

7. Vision

Purchase a watercolor set and some paper. Go out into nature, pick a scene, and to the best of your ability duplicate its image on the paper.

8. Fasting

For the period of 24 hours, do not eat. Drink only water or fruit and vegetable juices. If unable to fast, give up one food item for the day (i.e., coffee or soft drinks).

9. Separation

For the period of one night, sleep separately from your spouse or relationship partner. If you are alone, sleep in a different room of your home. Write down your experience before seeing your partner again.

Archangel
URIEL

365 Days

of Learning

& Appreciation

Archangel
URIEL

365 Days

of Learning

& Appreciation

Archangel
URIEL

365 Days

of Learning

& Appreciation

Archangel
URIEL

365 Days

of Learning

& Appreciation

Archangel
URIEL

365 Days

of Learning

& Appreciation

Archangel
URIEL

365 Days

of Learning

& Appreciation

Archangel
URIEL

365 Days

of Learning

& Appreciation

Archangel
URIEL

365 Days

of Learning

& Appreciation

Archangel
URIEL

365 Days

of Learning

& Appreciation

10.

Cleansing

For the period of 48 hours, do not bathe or shower (this is best done on a weekend).

11.

Cleaning

Wash one load of your laundry by hand in a wash tub or bath tub. Wring and hang dry.

12.

Electricity

For the period of 24 hours, do not use any small appliances that use electricity or batteries (such as tv or radio).

13.

Shower

Take one cold or cool shower.

14.

Writing

Write a letter to a loved one. Imagine that loved one is no longer on this earth. Say all your heart would long to say.

15.

Reading

Do not read anything intentionally for the period of 24 hours.

16.

Travel

Do not ride in a car, bus, motor vehicle, or bicycle for the period of 24 hours.

17.

Alone

Spend a day by yourself from sunrise to sunset. Make sure to get up in time to see the sunrise and watch the sunset. Do not do any form of work or entertainment for this whole period. Be with yourself.

18.

Surprise

Surprise a close friend, relative, or partner with something that you make. This could be food, a poem, or a gift of some other kind. Do not purchase this gift. You must make it.

Archangel
URIEL

365 Days

of Learning

& Appreciation

Archangel
URIEL

365 Days

of Learning

& Appreciation

Archangel
URIEL

365 Days

of Learning

& Appreciation

Archangel
URIEL

365 Days

of Learning

& Appreciation

Archangel
URIEL

365 Days

of Learning

& Appreciation

Archangel
URIEL

365 Days

of Learning

& Appreciation

Archangel
URIEL

365 Days

of Learning

& Appreciation

Archangel
URIEL

365 Days

of Learning

& Appreciation

Archangel
URIEL

365 Days

of Learning

& Appreciation

19.

Create your own

20.

Create your own

21.

Create your own

22.

Create your own

23.

Create your own

24.

Create your own

25.

Create your own

26.

Create your own

27.

Create your own